ROLL-UPS
& TEACUPS

ROLL-UPS & TEACUPS

Sylvia Whiteford-Engholm

MACMILLAN
LONDON

For my mother, my dearest friend,
and in loving memory of my father,
H. R. Whiteford-Engholm.
And for J.

First published 1990 by Macmillan London Limited, 4 Little Essex Street, London WC2R 3LF, and Basingstoke

Associated companies in Auckland, Delhi, Dublin, Gaborone, Hamburg, Harare, Hong Kong, Johannesburg, Kuala Lumpur, Lagos, Manzini, Melbourne, Mexico City, Nairobi, New York, Singapore and Tokyo

ISBN 0-333-52318-0
A CIP catalogue record for this book is available from the British Library

Designed by Robert Updegraff · Typeset by Wyvern Typesetting Limited, Bristol · Printed in Singapore

CONTENTS

ACKNOWLEDGEMENTS   7

A Hidden Westminster   8

First Impressions, 1947   12

Westminster Contrasts, 1948   24

A Generosity of Spirit, 1949   67

Kippers for Lunch, 1950   101

Dancing Down Old Pye Street, 1951   147

The Gold of the Sun, 1952   185

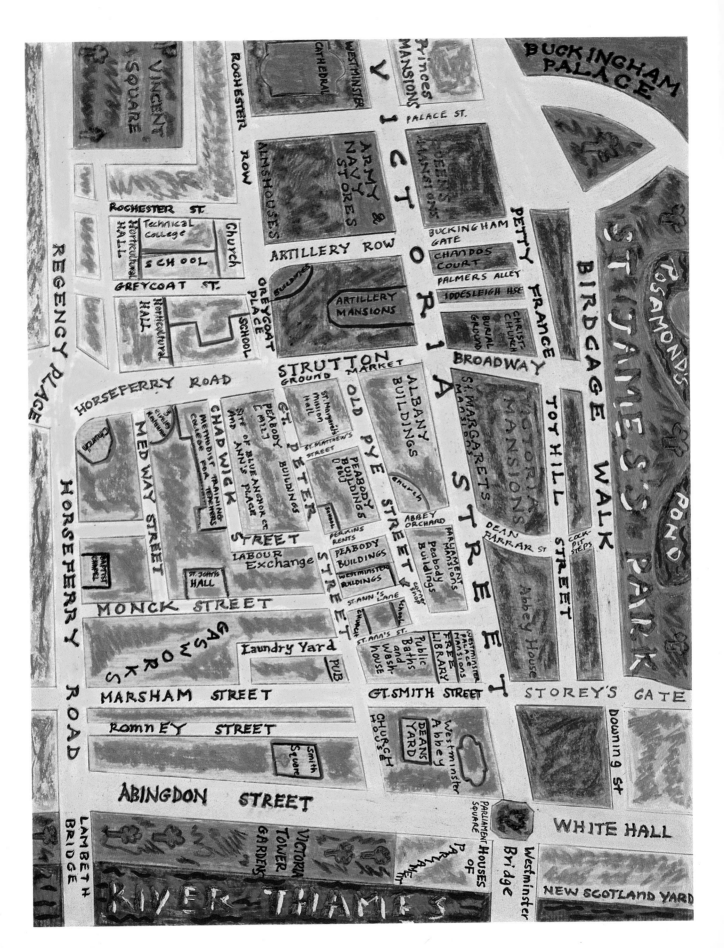

ACKNOWLEDGEMENTS

Marion West and David Whiteford-Engholm, whose excellent recall has allowed me to tap their first-hand knowledge, reminiscences and anecdotes of the period, which form the basis of this book.

My literary agent Patricia White; Lord Briggs, who headed the panel of judges for the competition organised by London Weekend Television in conjunction with the London History Workshop from which this book grew. Also Fay Weldon, Paul Thompson, Doc Rowe, Gemma Hunter, Carl Major and Liz Woodeson, Marion Milne of London Weekend Television, Susanna Wadeson of Macmillan, and Brenda Thomson.

Robert McCrum of Faber and Faber, for his initial encouragement and for pointing me in the right direction. Liz Calder of Bloomsbury Publishing, for her advice and encouragement. Warwick Charlton, writer and broadcaster, for his knowledge of and insight into the period of austerity. D. R. Williams for support and encouragement. Robert Updegraff, who designed the book.

The Reverend Jeremy Davies, a source of spiritual wealth and friendship in an inconstant world; and the Reverend Henry Dodd, Corpus Christi Church, Maiden Lane.

The Archive Department and staff of the City of Westminster Library, Buckingham Palace Road, whose collection of maps, photographs and other reference material proved invaluable. Also for the sense of industrious peace and calm of the British Library Reading Room in the British Museum, Bloomsbury, in which most of this was written.

Louisa Macqueeny, who has lived in Westminster for over eighty years, for her special and lifelong friendship. Also Maureen Synnak, Kathy Robinson, Maureen Brown and Mary O'Brien, in name for all those wonderful Westminster wives, mothers, sisters, aunts and children to whom this book pays warm tribute.

I am especially grateful to Kyle Cathie of Macmillan, fellow resident of Westminster, for her enthusiasm and courage in undertaking to publish this book.

A Hidden Westminster

The intention of this diary is to suggest something of the hardship and poverty of the period 1947–52 as encountered by a young mother, who, finding herself bombed out from her Belgravia mews home, is rehoused within the alluvial intimacy of a Westminster tenement.

Beginning towards the end of 1947, the diary attempts to capture something of the mood, tempo, emotion and texture of the tenement's grim day-to-day reality, woven around glimpses of some of the characters who gave it colour. It is a personal record of a bijou world; of how it was and how it felt. Ending in mid-1952 on the eve of the New Elizabethan Age, the Coronation and the plan to install electricity in the tenement, the diary does not look back to compare or with a sense of nostalgia. It was pretty awful then and still is in memory.

As the young mother, now in her mid-sixties, says:

Although it is behind me, the ghosts of its powerful imagery live on. To walk around these now more affluent streets, I am filled with a grim melancholy. Recalling the noise, laughter, quarrelling, kids shrieking and playing; the mothers, wives, grandmothers and aunts standing talking, going shopping, or trundling off to the local public baths with old prams and pushchairs piled with the weekly washing, over the cobblestones; their men grouped silently around the street-corners: visually little has changed, but the people have. Most of them are dead by now, or have moved on to better things. It appears to be smaller, even more enclosed, and I ask myself: did we really live there and was it really so hard? We did and it was.

> So dark is the dusk
> But not as much
> As my eye on show
> For poverty and hardship
> Are what I know
> How can I not recall
> Knowing what I know?

Looking back, it was a period that marked the arrival of the first privately owned car in the tenement, which was chased by a mass exodus of kids each time it entered the yard or drove off; saw the first refrigerator, with neighbours queueing for ice cubes; and even longer queues when a more enterprising neighbour had a telephone installed.

It was a time for listening to screaming kids, Cockney rhyming slang, drunken brawls, street-singing and the whistled tunes of Anne Shelton, Burl Ives, Jo Stafford and Nat King Cole; between honky-tonk piano sessions given by Winifred Attwell, a medley of tunes by Charlie Kunz and the *Blue Book of Jokes* by the Cheerful Chappie himself, Max Miller.

It was also a time when happiness was more readily obtainable, perhaps through finding lumps of coal left by the horse-driven deliveries; or finding loose tea in the grocer's discarded tea-chests; and finding boxes to chop up for firewood when the street-market closed for the day.

It was the period when the original Victoria Street existed intact, with its tired, yet continental-looking, hurried appearance — a street which three decades destroyed to replace with piles of blackening concrete and polluted glass. A period that had sought to destroy a century of respectable mansion blocks, shops, restaurants and a department store within the precinct of St James's Park, Westminster Abbey, Westminster Cathedral, Buckingham Palace and the façade splendours of Belgravia.

The only street colour was supplied by red buses, neon signs, ice-cream parlours, milk bars, pillar boxes and telephone kiosks, together with the sandwich-board men, whose calligraphy, adverts and hieroglyphs loaned a picturesque tonality to the scene. And when the shop-window displays were stacked rather than arranged, filled rather than displayed with tins, fruit packets, tubs, pots, bottles and boxes. When the old sniffed snuff, sipped tea and sat with their memories, burning paper and rags in the grate for warmth.

It was a period when money was scarce, pleasures few, and a major escape came in the form of a wireless set or a Reader's Ticket for the Great Smith Street Public Library.

And when night fell and the various Lyons', ABC and Express teashops were closed, there were always the all-night coffee stalls selling their distillations of coffee essences, mugs of steaming tea, cocoa and heated pies with lashings of brown sauce, to ease something of the gloom, fog, rain and loneliness in urban Westminster.

Quiet, austere-looking and composed stands a heavy, brickwork pile whose harsh appearance confirms its mid-Victorian separateness in faded and threadbare streets. A street near a pub whose atmosphere hangs heavy with ash and alcohol; and three rooms, one of which is lit by incandescence. Three windows for three rooms, once home for a mother, husband and child.

Although based on recollections of the period, the characters and events described in this book are fictional.

Victoria Street

Opposite   *'The dingiest collection of shabby buildings ever squeezed together in a rank corner as a club for tom cats.'* – *Charles Dickens,* Household Words.

First Impressions

1947

Westminster sw1
Night tones

Amber Indigo and Rust
Clove, Mushroom
Cinnamon and Grape

Beyond St James's Park and Victoria Station lies a richly contrasting world where the night-time prowlers are in evidence; a jostle of people who may never come together. But it is not the season, nor the fascia's tone or colour, which contains Westminster's essence of being as a haunting linkwork of streets whose ambience lives on its own terms.

November 19th The moon was low again last night, tipping something of its mystery and light over the rooftops. It is over three years since Roland and I were bombed out of Ebury Mews and moved into Nos. 33–5 Chesham Place, originally a halfway home, along with others in our predicament. The post this morning brought an offer of accommodation in a tenement block in Westminster, behind the Army and Navy Stores. Three rooms, it said. A living room, two bedrooms, with a shared WC and cold running water tap along a passage. I hope it is clean. Bugs don't make class distinctions.

I like the night hours. The night hides, heightens, detracts, exposes and distorts the harder images of day. It arrives gradually, almost imperceptibly, as the shades become shadows that are more subtle, variable, more mysterious. Night-time, I decide, might prove a better time for viewing the rooms.

We are walking a little this side of black. Longing for joy, a touch of colour, anything to change it to hope. I picked up the weekly grocery ration from Pearks' store this afternoon. As usual Mary managed to put in an extra $\frac{1}{4}$ lb of tea and a tin of condensed milk. Last week it was extra butter, and before that, sugar. What a brick she is always, the quick smile or joke as she packs my bag. One often finds the experience of hardship can bring out a special kindness and sympathy in people. The day goes on and the threat of winter's arrival does nothing to alleviate my increasing sense of doom as I decide to look over the rooms. As Roland is in Denham at the film studios, extraing this week, I will have to go alone with Sally, who is nine months old, in the pram.

Roland, with his canvases and celluloid life, is the realist among those other post-war insular romantics. As darkness swallows me up, he remains haunted by the starkness of the reality before him. The imagery of streets, nocturnes of city life; the ever-changing room interiors in which he withdraws to create. But he is not strong. He smokes too much, in an attitude of preference to hide his sense of inadequacy and failure. At least Mother was happy at my news.

November 20th I woke with a start this morning, aware this was the day to go and view the rooms. It was not quite six, so I lay for a moment looking down at Sally asleep in her basket. Observing Roland's layers of white handkerchiefs, screwed paper notes, sketches and a dish of cigarette ends along the window sill, like a testimony to lost times. After lunch I made the journey on foot from Lyall Street. Walking among people hunched against the wind and sky, whose thundery tones threatened to enclose us. Some had formed bus queues along Buckingham Palace Road. Cold-looking and forlorn as tombs waiting to be lit with colour. In the distance lies Victoria Street. A long and windy strip of a thoroughfare, lit by gas and sprinkled with fine shops. Its offices and mansion blocks and stone Government piles loom before us like anaesthetised remains from a previous epoch. It is a pleasure to look in the windows and observe the arrangements of merchandise. Powders, perfumes, lipsticks and pots alongside well-made garments in a variety of textures.

In Artillery Row I stop for a cup of tea in the Express Dairy to give myself strength and an opportunity to feed Sally. In spite of the hour, it was full of people sheltering from the wind. From my window seat I could see civil servants walking, bowler-hatted and with rolled umbrellas, and various other office workers going about their business; walking and working in the awareness of today. Turning the corner where the Artillery Buildings links with Greycoat Place, I got lost in a drab network of streets. I have never visited this neighbourhood before, running at right-angles to Victoria Street.

Named 'the Devil's Acre' by Charles Dickens in his weekly journal, *Household Words*, in 1857, it is a district embroiled in a West End momentum. Reality, Roland once said, is that split second between observer and observed. And this is it. This was it. I am here but not here, watching myself look. Turning into a street of silent, curtained windows, with dark alleys, dustbins and shadows, the reality I see is of an environment asleep in itself. A film set awaiting a new location or an inspired director to order it back to life. Walking towards the tenement, I am guided towards a brick arch behind a bomb site. The legacy of war is evident, with many examples of shored-up walls, corrugated metal, rubble and desolation. Even Sally looked startled. First impressions are the most accurate, before imagination and sentiment step in to cover up the cracks. Every stone, brick, leaf, ragwort and daisy seemed rooted to its own selected space.

*The Abbey coffee stall, standing on the site of the bombed Westminster
Hospital where I went for treatment as a child.*

There was a bomb site surrounded by grim, austere blocks aligned with children's hopscotch markings, cobbles, derelict doorways and grime. In silence I find our destination, locate the duty porter who gives me the key, and we make our way over the courtyard towards a block entrance painted brown and cream. I am conscious of concrete, worn steps, the marking-time faces of the inhabitants peering curiously at us. The shapes gathering around us in the fast-approaching dark. It was quite a shock. Do people really live in here, I thought? If this was reality, when would the dream begin?

There are places, as there are people, whose powerful personality and character can remain imprinted forever. And this would be one of them. I felt as though I were entering a living page from John Hollingshead's *Ragged London*, with its opportunities for collision and confrontation in its court-like approach; its rooms, passages and wash-houses, which have produced a physical testament of share and share alike.

I wore black. People wear a lot of black these days. Black pulls in the contours and can become a disguise. It can single out or render one invisible. Above all it is easy to wear and can look chic when having to dress on a small budget. On reflection, it was most appropriate for the visit.

'You'll be all right in here,' the porter said. 'This block didn't get bombed. Built to last, these are. The walls are six bricks deep in parts.'

'It's a bit on the dark side,' I replied. 'I'd hoped for a lighter place, especially with a baby.'

'They were going to put you upstairs, but that had to be fumigated at the last moment.'

We all have our moments of alienation. The overpowering sense of isolation when standing in a strange street or a strange place. Moments when we attempt to distract ourselves from a sense of emptiness. My distraction was to lift Sally from her pram and give her a hug.

November 23rd Tea tonight will have to be a slice of Hovis bread spread with a ration of margarine and sugar; there is not anything else. We have to go easy on bread since it was rationed in July of last year. Especially with potatoes now added to the list.

We are blanketed in fog, which reminds me of the war, when London really did disappear and go underground. Roland longs for some Mediterranean light to mix on his canvases. He is at the studios, working on David Lean's *Great Expectations*, so his hours are getting filled. I find myself reminding him that time, our time especially, is unredeemable and that we have to make the most of what we have.

November 24th Well, I have taken a look. Have taken up the challenge, so to speak, and accepted their offer.

'You can take it or leave it,' they said. 'There are plenty more waiting in the queue.' The Council never makes more than one offer.

Roland, who did not want to lose a day's filming money, had left the decision to me. We had to live somewhere and, with luck, it might not be for long. War with its curses, I thought. That we should be reduced to this. Roland sees it differently.

'Look at those Haussman apartments in Paris, which are also built around a courtyard,' he said. 'Close your eyes and pretend these are the same. At least they are functional and built to fulfil a necessary purpose.'

Living in them will prove otherwise. He felt it to have a sinister beauty. A certain rustic façade which socially separates itself from the surrounding environment, community and streets. Poor Roland. But I know what he means. There is this front world of appearance, which encloses a darker, and infinitely more real one. A tenement world which is largely unseen. A prison, I call it. Complete with railings, regimented brickwork, iron bars, cobblestones and cells.

So this is it. This is our window and this is to be our view, and for who knows how long. To cheer me up, my brother Freddie made me a copy of Matisse's *Still Life with Oysters*. Blue for despair, red for rage and yellow for hope, I thought.

Do people really live here?

Opposite   *As far as I can see, the only colour in the tenement seems to
come from the fabric of the women's frocks and aprons.*

November 28th There has not been much sewing work recently and the continuing clothes couponing does little to help our plight. The *Evening News* stated that Princess Elizabeth was granted a bonus issue of coupons for her wedding dress. I wondered how they managed the reception with so many food items rationed.

'Come on,' Mother pointed out later, in response to my grumbles. 'It could be worse. Think of those poor souls with no roof over their heads. You can make it nice. Place your things. Run up some pretty curtains. You'll see.'

We will see indeed. Roland and a crowd from the film set paid a visit to Muriel Belcher's place in Soho, the Colony, where she allowed them champagne on tick, or so they said.

December 1st So what do we get for a weekly rent of 7/3d? For a start the building is a warren of staircases and corridors, which open *en suite* to rooms set at intervals along cream, distempered passageways. Each black street-door has its own identifying number and brass knocker. Ours is No. 60. Tiny, these regimental, brickworked suites of rooms each has an iron range, and a wooden cupboard for both food and coal. Each suite, with its incandescent lighting, represents a spectacle of gloom and hardship. Tinged with fog and bare floorboards, they still compete with their Victorian ancestors for survival. Tenement blocks, I tell myself, in which the elemental gloom seems to pervade the walls, windows, clothes and pores of our bodies; enclosing our brains, desires and hopes.

Maybe I exaggerate. Claudine, my sister, says I do. She thought it could be made cosy and, if I organised my bottom-drawer collection, plus a ready supply of kettles, pots and jugs to avoid unnecessary journeys to and from the communal tap, I would be all right. 'At least it's your own little place,' she said, 'where you can plan your day, do more or less as you please.' It was Claudine who wanted to know about the neighbours, who they were, what they were like and where they were from.

'We have to forget the war. Forget the way it destroyed everything, altered many of our destinies.' She is right, of course. There are things we must put behind us. Roland, Sally and I are in the here and now.

The Utility furniture has arrived. I ordered it from a catalogue range and stored it in a garage in the mews. It did not seem much at the time but, in here, it makes the room look overcrowded. I have my treddle Singer sewing machine in front of the window, the large kitchen table in the centre, the two armchairs either side of the grate, and the chest of drawers by the wall. I did not have enough coupons for a sideboard. There is a high chair for Sally, two kitchen chairs and a stool. We have to breathe in as we ease ourselves from one part of the room to another.

It seems a little unreal, this room.

December 14th Roland arrived back from the film earlier today carrying a pot of black-market jam. Something to add to the usual slice of Hovis bread, he said. He never says much about his work, except to point out that either he is standing in for Derek Bond, Stewart Granger or David Niven, or that his time is spent in the fantasy world which lends support to his ideas and inspirations.

'We are all between living and half-living,' he says, 'attempting to pick up the pieces of our scattered lives.' But I wonder if we are? As each of us assembles a shelter in which to arrange our eating, sleeping and talking. And for those in Roland's mould, a little play-acting too!

He goes out for some space and I am left in it. It is early days yet, but there is no escape for me staring at these four walls, except to pause within their isolated patches, or go down the passage to the loo, or draw water for the kettle. These dark Westminster contrasts support this tedium and tedious life. When he is in, he invariably sleeps, closing his eyes to the immediate world around him. Or sits coughing; those moments when he, too, seems to be disorientated and divided by a sense of loss. The spiritual loss of his day, his life with its ideas snuffed out by war.

December 26th We spent our first Christmas in the tenement, and the third of our marriage, apart. Roland went to Putney and Sally and I to Lyall Mews. With no coal, money or energy, it was thought best to enjoy the festive season with our respective parents. Roland's mother is very ill, spending her wakeful hours sitting in a corner, draped in blankets.

My brother Freddie and I hung paperchains and streamers cut out of paper bought from Woolworth's. On Christmas Eve we walked back from King's Road in the pale sunlight, discovering this and pointing out that. In spite of the season the area was quiet, with little evidence of last-minute shopping. An hour in which the shabby stucco, blitzed squares and craters of Belgravia appeared temporarily hung with gold.

I bought a box of Max Factor face-powder and a Yardley's cherry-red lipstick. I like Woolworth's, with its infinite variety of products, bustling activity, partitioned counters and bare wooden floorboards which acknowledge my platform-heeled shoes. The manager went about his work whistling 'Maybe it's because I'm a Londoner' and offered me a glass of lemonade from the bubbling glass vat on the corner of the sweets counter. Sipping it gratefully, I looked out at the King's Road with its sense of tomorrow, the New Year, its red buses, black taxi cabs all going zroom zroom, broom zroom.

Today I walked back to No. 60 with Sally in the pram. My second sister, Patricia, came with me to stay for a few days, as Roland plans to remain with his mother for the rest of the week. Patricia adores taking Sally to the park while I get on with the chores. Everywhere we looked, evidence of war loomed uppermost. Fragments of buildings, derelict and boarded-up shops, and torn-apart houses littered the scene like a clutter of crumpled photographs on a mantelshelf.

*Agnes Tillett – Old Mother Stout-Guzzler, always drunk
and tripping over the gutters while talking to herself, the
local cats and pigeons.*

Agnes Tillett knocked on the door around 3.30 with two slices of her home-made Christmas cake. She had seen us crossing the yard. She stayed an hour, illuminating for us the mysteries of life in the tenement.

'Most have lived here for years. None of us has any money. We wouldn't be here if we did.' I don't agree with that. I think most would choose to live here even if they were millionaires, because they enjoy this close community life where each is seen to live virtually within the others' pockets. Patricia listened intently while I rearranged the wall-cupboard in the bedroom. There was a smell of damp in there, penetrating my linens and dress fabrics, which were stacked in it.

WESTMINSTER
CONTRASTS
1948

January 26th It is all cut-backs and rationing these days. First it was the wartime shortages and now it is peacetime privations, black-market deals and spivs. Cartoons depict them as thin, moustached individuals with slit eyes and wide-brimmed, slouch hats, men who wear jackets with wide padded shoulders. There are a few standing on the corner of St Matthew's Street. The four o'clock post brought an element of unexpected cheer in the form of two crisp pound notes and a rag-book of nursery rhymes for Sally. A woman I made a wedding dress for last year sent it as a gesture of goodwill and to celebrate the pending arrival of her first child.

'Nothing lasts, when you think about it,' said Roland this morning, 'except the lastingness of things.' He was feeling optimistic and philosophical, although he is without film-work since completing *The Odd Man Out*. He is missing the film set's cafeteria talk and camaraderie shared by those other emotional narcotics. I made a pot of tea, cut slices of Christmas cake, while a pot of rabbit stew warmed on the range. And for a while we sat and talked in the firelight. Exchanges of memories, those pre-war reminiscences, as Mr Lamplighter-Biker, as Roland calls him, cycled past.

I managed to hold on to those wartime radio recipes which advised us how to make do with too little food. Talks given by Baron Woolton entitled *The Kitchen Front*. I thought of inviting one of the neighbours in to join us, like old Frederick Scullion from down the passage. I met him in Pearks, the grocer's, last Friday, the poor old soul shuffling along in the rations' queue. He looked so pale and thin amid the sawdust in a pair of old army boots. He seemed delighted when I bid him hello. 'Always time for a pretty face,' he said.

February 12th There is a pub at the top of the street which is a local hang-out for writers, comedians and other up-and-coming radio personalities; and by no means least for the tenants. A lively domain from which I see neighbours emerging at intervals with jugs of draught beer from the Jug and Bottle Bar to take home. In the gutter nearby a

woman lies drunk. At any moment two stalwarts will arrive on the scene to haul her to her feet. The smell of her time-ravaged guts sticks to her hair and clothes. Marie Flynn lives upstairs with her daughter June, the early-morning newspaper-round girl. For most of the time, so my neighbour Jean Farmer tells me, Marie and June make do. But occasionally, and especially of a Friday night, the membrane ruptures, separating the real world from the non-real; it all gets a bit too much and solace is sought. A pale face lies sleepless, waiting for Marie Flynn to come home, listening to the sounds of laboured sex upstairs. The bang-banging of the iron bed against the wall, the kids whose cries go unheeded, and the row next door over money, debt and betrayal. Each in turn revealing our basic lack of privacy.

Mr Cornelius Wilby, a once sought-after gossip-column luminary, sleeps on regardless, locked between mementoes of his former cocktail, caviare and gilt-edged days in this threadbare wilderness. A family of five are attempting to sleep on two mattresses spread over the floor, fighting for life, breath and oxygen beneath damp-patched walls. The even shapes of the street-lights break through the curtains to catch my imagination like open teeth that threaten to consume. My mind travels around the narrow strips of streets, the market with its fruit and vegetable stalls, public baths down the alley. The people gathering in groups to talk, who cast doleful glances over those others with time to spare. And sleep won't come to help alleviate this night with its interior darkness.

The Brylcreem and moustache give the spiv away.

Opposite   *The Grafton, a den of iniquity – we never go there.*

February 14th This seems to be it. The nights are getting lighter and Roland says to me, 'Take it easy, it can't last.' But it does. We have no money, no savings and, therefore, no means of escape. I don't always see it this way, but today I do.

To make matters worse, Mother bumped into Jeremy yesterday in Cliveden Place. Tall, lean and aquiline, with the looks of a matinée idol, she has always liked him. He is now studying medicine. 'A worthwhile profession,' she said. 'You should have married him when you had the chance instead of throwing your life away on some artist–dreamer-cum-actor.'

I dated Jeremy for a little while in the days before I met Roland. But who can say whether or not our feelings might have turned to love? Whether life with him might have been better? It would have been different certainly, with a man I admired, liked but did not love.

'Who needs art?' Mother asks. 'Art and play-acting won't feed you and your child in these austere days.'

Roland should have linked with Nash, Minton and Henry Moore, along with others from his period. He knew them, used to linger around their drug and Benzedrine, café-pub haunts from time to time. Those Fitzrovia and Soho bohemian pursuits of the literary–art fraternity. He was offered a teaching post at the Slade, where he was a student, but he declined. It was simple pride. Something about 'only those who can't, teach'; that it is the real failures who need the security of the payroll. He could have applied to become an Official War Artist, thereby guaranteeing a measure of recognition and employment. His excuse was, mysteriously, 'We are viewing from different focal points.' He seems to have found an appreciative ear in Cornelius Wilby in K Block. Mr Wilby keeps a secret supply of sweets in a tin box – so the neighbours say in conspiratorial undertones. Locally, he is referred to as the Sweet Man. He goes about his days wearing a trilby hat. 'There goes old Wilby wearing his trilby,' the neighbourhood kids chant, calling on him for sherbet-dabs, bull's-eyes, fruit gums, peppermints: anything to quench an immediate craving for sugar. He must have a secret access to sweep coupons from the Ministry of Food. Roland likes him because he knew Noël Coward and can extol the virtues of living beneath a Cap Ferrat sun. And can speak of Graham Sutherland's painterly love-affair with the Mediterranean culture.

'Massine and Helpman are over there now,' he told Roland, 'choreographing and dancing with Moira Shearer in Michael Powell's film–poem, *The Red Shoes*.' A comment which left Roland even more unsettled in this winter gloom.

February 17th The tenement is very much an island-like community centred within each connecting block, inhabited by sets of intricate kinship networks spanning several generations.

'Her mother next door lived here. Her mother before her. And her old man's sister married the plumber in D Block, and his cousin married her aunt.'

Living within bare plastered walls, whose monotony of cream, pale-green or khaki distemper remains unrelieved by pretence or ornament. Chars, cooks and costers, nurses, butchers, carpenters, labourers, printers, shoemakers, seamstresses, tailors, packers and messengers.

Sally is asleep as I walk the pram through the park. There is a temporary feeling of freedom beneath this pale, saffron sky. A man passing smiles, so I smile back. It is considered bad form to admit being lonely. One must be seen to cope, because others can't cope with one's loneliness, lest it force their own emotions to the surface. Usually no one looks at me, nor I at them. An odd life. Me in this thin coat, well-washed floral frock and wedge-heeled sandals with a hole in the right sole. Two office girls, feeding the ducks from their lunch-packs on the suspension bridge, are discussing what they are going to wear tonight at the dance in Caxton Hall. It is a long time since I went to a dance, wore scent or 'planned my outfit'. Roland has three left feet so we usually sat them out.

March 2nd I like to get up early to enjoy my first cup of tea in silence. To sit quietly with my cup and a dry biscuit before Roland and Sally stir. When Roland is on location, or working at Denham, he has to get up first. I look around and absorb something of the vagueness and muted colours. It is not really dark and nor is it light, and to see what I am doing is a strain. Frederick Scullion's got a bad cough. Rose Sweeny, the Toffee-Apple Woman, was knocking on his door on Sunday to see how he was. There is an element of care and caring here, which is good. Alec, our friendly Scottish milkman, often bangs on a door if he's not seen its occupant in a couple of days, to see that all is well. And nothing ever gets missed by Violet Clixby, Mrs Streetwatcher, forever leaning out of her window, seeing all that there is to see. The Playfoot Dairy and the United Dairies in Strutton Ground supply most of the milk delivered here, sending out roundsmen with pullalong carts. And there goes Wilfred Twaddle, the Lamplighter-Biker, ringing his bicycle bell to catch Mabel Wagstaffe's attention on the ground floor. I fancy there is a little spring and twinkle in the air, there.

March 17th Albert Mavrolean from two doors down has started working in the Army and Navy Stores Wine Department and suggested Roland should look for temporary work there too. 'They give a free glass of wine each day,' he said. 'Give him a bit of colour.'

I manage to get a few sewing and alteration jobs here and there; most comprise complete unpicking and remaking to stretch into new ways. It is hardly the class of garment I was handling at William Hartnell's or Woolland's in Knightsbridge before the war. As soon as it was discovered around here that I could do dressmaking, I was inundated with requests. Although I doubt many could afford to pay and that would lead to complications.

I took Sally to the park today because Roland noticed the daffodils were in bloom. Crossing the Birdcage Walk we could see carpets and carpets of them greeting the sun. Gazing across the lake, I was conscious of mood, the sun and the strangely equinoctial nature of things, and felt reassured. That sense of peace and confirmation one has when standing in the presence of beauty.

Mrs Hicks's old man has abandoned her for another woman, so Jean Farmer tells me. The poor woman was beside herself with grief. She has been left with four children to feed. Madam Spinster Lonely-Heart, as Roland refers to Alice Underwood, was soon on the scene with platefuls of salt-and-vinegar chip commiserations. To be rejected or betrayed is a terrible pain. One worse than facing death, I think. She was better off without a man like that, the neighbours said. No matter who we are, the emotion of love touches us all in one way or another. Tomorrow I will tackle the spring-cleaning and emulate the Job-Boys from the local Scout pack. I will make a start on the curtains, cushions and the knitted rugs. Polish the framed reproduction of Rome with its street-scene of Bernini's baroque façades. Even Rome has its sea of anonymous faces, which become a variable blur.

The hour and the sun move on apace, spotlighting the cracks, holes and crevices set deep into folds of green distemper. Then I knock over a tin of self-raising flour which I am using to rub in a few cakes. The nights are still cold, the streets gloomy-looking and contained until the lamplighter ignites them, isolating the gas-lamps in their own shadowy perimeters.

Before bed I found myself thinking of Mrs Hicks and her sad predicament. I wonder what makes love die, or start for that matter? All these people relating, equating and separating. And what of those who stay, the ones who are left behind? The ones who are left to pick up the pieces? It is sad for the love which lingers regardless. I took comfort in one of Stiles' eccles cakes and a cup of weak tea.

March 20th Poor Roland. In spite of those thoughts of Haussman and those Paris apartment blocks, he is finding it difficult to adjust to the squalor after all. He escapes from it as much as he can with walks around town; seeking solace in Victoria Street, the parks, Piccadilly and Shaftesbury Avenue. He spends hours smoking roll-ups and drinking tea in a Cranbourn Street cellar or one of the numerous ABC, Express or Lyons' teashops. On one particularly dull Sunday, he bought a 1d platform ticket at Victoria and sat amid the steam, observing a host of arrivals and departures. No doubt he was mentally travelling with them. And for 2d, he spent another day going twice round the Inner Circle on the Underground, entering by St James's Park and later alighting at Westminster.

I have the impression that some of the neighbours view us with suspicion. I heard one commenting to Agnes Tillett, who loyally spoke up for us, 'They shouldn't be here, people like that,' followed by, 'We're every bit as good as them.'

It isn't that we have gone out of our way to be stand-offish; simply that anyone who is different from the norm, by way of appearance, experience and background, has difficulty being accepted. There is always a divide. But we are by no means alone in our predicament and isolation. There are others whose reduced circumstances have forced them into these unaccustomed and desperate conditions. No one should have to walk down a long passage to fetch water, or have to visit a loo shared by goodness knows whom. We keep our WC locked to prevent those from the street using it. But not everyone is so diligent, especially when the keys get lost.

Roland's increasing separateness, his and mine together which separates us from them, leaves me in the somewhat precarious role of onlooker. Someone unable to halt the march of time. It is especially difficult for Roland because he grew up in the more gentle world of nannies, servants and prep. school. Now he is reduced to washing from a chipped enamel bowl balanced on an ironing board. His crucifix and rosary beads hang prominently from a hook by the bed, together with a yellowing pile of the *Tablet* reminding the observer and himself of his faith. I wonder on occasions who the real Roland is. Now he is out of work. The actor who is forever acting. But he is nevertheless kind, sensitive, witty and cultured, if not on occasions a trifle bizarre. Memories of Barnes, trips on the Golden Arrow to Paris, the Pullman carriage to Brighton with whispered confidences of courtship and rendezvous on Putney Common at dusk, help sustain him.

We had herrings rolled in oatmeal with mashed potato for tea tonight, while the wireless played 'The Way You Looked Tonight', setting us on a pace or two.

It is pleasant to dress to the still warm embers in the grate.

March 22nd Such a pale dawn to provide a camouflage for this over-inhabited world. A thinly disguised momentum in which the bombed Mission Hall of the Good Shepherd opposite our windows separates us from the sun. When I think Eaton Square used to be my garden and Belgrave Square my park, I feel inexorably sad. But it is the second day of spring and we are close to that magnificent park, St James's, with its lake, sandpit and swings for Sally when she is older, and its seasonal contrasts for me.

I like to cut two thin slices of bread and spread them with a little marmalade in the mornings. One for myself, and one for Roland to eat with his tea. We have such an uncomplicated diet. It must be a bore to be rich and so spoiled for choice. But this morning he does not appear to be hungry, preferring to draw heavily on a roll-up in bed instead. He was coughing again well into the night, keeping me awake. He gets up next to wait for the kettle to boil, stopping to rinse his face and cup in a bowl of tepid water on the ironing board. Soap comes in a bar of carbolic; the towel is draped over the brass fireguard for warmth. He places his clothing on a stool and I leave him in privacy. It is his day for the Labour Exchange in Chadwick Street; the film-work appears to have dried up completely. He walked all the way to Putney High Street last night after dinner to see if he could get an evening job as doorman at the Putney Regal. With the night air being fresh, he did not notice how tired he was. He just kept on going, along the New King's

· 35 ·

Road, past the Chelsea Ritz Cinema, the workhouse buildings and Chelsea Palace, into the darkness.

With Easter on the horizon, the tenement kids are out in their hundreds, chalking up seasonal hopscotch and rounders markings in primary colours. 'Those latter-day Mondrians', Roland calls them, in reference to the gridlines and colours used for these particular pastimes. Playing games of 'He', Knock-Down-Ginger, skipping and scootering on home-made contraptions with ball-bearings and planks of wood. To get from the White Arch entrance to our block requires some sure-footed manoeuvres. From our side of the White Arch there are five block entrances. In front of each are groups of women: wives, mothers, sisters, girlfriends and grandmothers stand talking. They stand mob-capped and aproned, with both arms and legs folded, invariably propping up a window-sill or wall. One leans against a pushchair piled with clean washing; another smokes. Above them, faces lean from windows, calling out to one another with words of greeting, gossip, or simple acknowledgement. They represent an excursion into texture, foundation, the security of certainty. The simple joy of lives caught briefly in an act of communication. This is Pieter Bruegel's *Children's Games*, 1560, re-enacted in Westminster, 1948.

Walking through a spring St James's Park with Sally, I forget the discomfort and loneliness, the narrowness and intolerance. What happens when feelings of isolation and alienation close in within this inauspicious pocket of London? The wooden suspension bridge over the lake, the crocuses and daffodils; the ice-cream café in the market with hot bread from the baker's: the preciseness of them all awakens in us the sudden discovery of seeing things we already know.

Even Bessie Fonseca smiled as we entered the block: 'All right, love?' she asked. 'Soon be walking, eh? Love her'; a smile and a comment suggesting a level of complicity, which, if I so desired, I could pursue. But I was gasping for a cup of tea.

I left Sally with a box of lids and saucepans, crawling on the floor while I placed the kettle over the gas.

Seasonal notes

Pale sun half circumferenced
by gold, bronze and oyster.
Those mauve, yellow and white crocuses
springing so gloriously into life

March 28th It was so cold last night I could not sleep. I would like to light a fire in the bedroom, but with the room being small and the end of the bed inches from it, it wouldn't be safe. I thought we were in for a repeat of last winter, when snowdrifts of up to fifteen feet high were reported, when magazines were suspended and daily newspapers reduced to four pages. The news was so bleak it was a wonder people wanted to read them anyway.

Katrina, Roland's mother, died yesterday afternoon. We had never been more than passing acquaintances. She had resented my taking away her first-born son; mothers can be very possessive of their sons. Once an actress on the London stage, she had retained evidence of her former beauty and dignity. I never saw her anywhere other than sitting in a corner of the room. Her composure and Edwardian gentility seeking privacy behind a veil. An eclectic spirit, her once gay façade hid the nervous solicitude and pain of a woman who was dying. I won't be going to the funeral. Roland and Dominic will attend with Henry, their father. Three tall, thin men, fatigued of life in their collective search for recognition. Each remembering a love made luxuriant in words and form. Writing poetry, acting and canvases, those gentle reminders of a once vibrant, yet fast-changing world.

I read somewhere that peace and happiness in a relationship come from giving up trying to find them. They are not something people can give you publicly, to be worn like a frock or suit. Roland has faith. I entertain doubts, but then I am of a more practical leaning. We both have our secret places in which to site our secret thoughts. He did not say anything when he came home, but simply picked over his food and retreated into the bedroom. After a pause I could hear him going through his suitcases with their contents of papers and documents. Unfolding and refolding letters and clicking them shut. Death breaks something intact and can only be survived by letting go.

'Faith is a secret we all have access to,' said Roland later. 'But it is one most of us have lost.'

Tomorrow I will go and light a candle in St Ann's; sit for a while in its dark enclosure.

March 30th The priest from St Ann's Church in Old Pye Street made himself known the other night and stayed for a cup of tea. He had seen us in church and had taken the opportunity to welcome us to the parish, albeit six months on. He came largely to remind us that it was Lent and of our obligations. What with Roland being a lapsed Catholic, our poverty and my doubt, the prospect of unplanned pregnancies, talk of prayer, penance and almsgiving are not what we wish to hear right now. He was a large man with black hair. Roland got into a heated argument over something or other, so I busied myself making a pot of tea.

Roland told the priest how he had once received a call to the priesthood.

'You should have answered it,' he replied.

'I did,' replied Roland. 'I said no and married Veronica.'

'That was a blasphemy. A call is a God-given privilege, a grace directed to a few.'

'It was not anything visible, invisible or coherent, something I could define,' Roland continued regardless, 'it was something I came to recognise with an instinctive foreknowledge. A feeling which presented no mystery to me.'

'And you said no?'

'Sometimes you have to say no. One does not necessarily know why. Maybe Sally will make amends one day.'

I feel embarrassed when guests are here, having to prepare sandwiches or tea in front of them. The blocks in Horseferry Road have tiny brown-and-white-tiled kitchenettes, which offer a measure of culinary privacy, even if too small to eat in. Those blocks went up in 1922 when Blue Anchor Court and Ann's Place were demolished. Old Emily Riggs who plays the barrel-organ on Saturday mornings by the corner of Chadwick Street told me she grew up there. 'If you think people are hard up now, dearies,' she said, 'you should have seen how we lived then.'

I woke early this morning with an unexpected feeling of happiness. It is strange how one can sometimes, and for no reason other than that it is spring. We live in a secret world here. A world largely unseen by those living and working in adjoining streets and thoroughfares. Few walking down Victoria Street or Whitehall, or beside those elegant mansion blocks near the Westminster Cathedral and Westminster Palace Gardens, would anticipate finding us here. Even I had not known before that this milieu existed. A world running between layers of grey, levels of distemper, and contrasts.

Later, when I collected the sheets and towels from the Sunlight Laundry in Horseferry Road, I bought my quarterly copy of *Modern Living* from the Gas-Light and Coke Company's showrooms a few doors down. I had some coupons left and bought 3 oz of Sharpes's toffees from Redding's, the sweetshop in Marsham Street, walking by way of Laundry Yard. Badly bombed, hardly a shop remains in Marsham Street, which was once like a village in itself. Sandwiched between the King's Head public house at one end and the Queen's Head at the other, stood a variety of shops, cafés and small businesses, which included a cats' meat shop, printers, drapers, chemist and fried-fish shop.

Bennett's Yard, linking Romney Street with Marsham, was once a row of cottages, but since the Blitz it is a weed-growing garden whose remaining walls are shored against the Abbey Community Centre. In Smith Square stands the badly bombed shell of St John the Evangelist, which, with Christchurch in Victoria Street and St Andrew's in Ashley Place, took a direct hit during a night-time air-raid.

My favourite part of Westminster is the area around Dean's Yard and Barton Street, and I often find myself walking this way. Streets which Roland says are wholly distinctive by their ageless calm, red brick and iron railings. Streets at once exclusive and inclusive, in contrast to those enclosing the tenement. I know what my sister Claudine means about being lucky to live in SW1. There is much to appreciate and value, and all free.

I have not been feeling well this week, so Roland has had to play cook and host. He really has no idea. Comes of being waited on by servants and now me. He has lived on Shredded Wheat, toast and boiled eggs all the week. I sat and watched him at teatime, going about the one thing he can really do, and that is make a good pot of tea. Lighting the gas beneath the kettle and arranging the cups and saucers on the table before pouring the boiling water into the pot. Sipping the hot tea, revived by its sweetness, he studied the design on the Shredded Wheat box. Empty, they make useful storage boxes. Sally has one for her crayons and rag-books, and I have one for my notepaper and receipts. Roland keeps notes and jottings in another. Scraps of order and disorder which focus his intelligence. With the assistance of a long fork I toasted bread by the fire and, eating margarine-covered toast and sipping tea, we settled down to listen to a serial on *Children's Hour*. The neighbours were quiet for once and later, when I went down to the rubbish chute in my dressing gown, most of the curtains were drawn against the dark. An environment asleep in itself, as one might say.

'That priest shouldn't have gone on so,' said Roland at length. 'It wasn't for him to judge my decision, but God.'

'I shouldn't worry about it. Perhaps he's regretting answering his own call,' I said. 'It's an unnatural life for a man.'

'It sets them apart, the celibacy. I knew from childhood I wanted to be a priest. There was this knowledge that one's life was somehow already charted and fixed.'

'Except free will,' I answered. 'We have free will to change things.' I wish I believed that. If I did we would not be sitting in front of the fire sipping tea. 'Besides, one is always a priest. It is as intact as one's soul, integrity and character, no matter what one does later.'

I wasn't sure what I meant by that, but it silenced Roland. He says that tomorrow morning he will go to the Cathedral for Mass.

April 2nd I woke this morning with a smell of soot in my nose and mouth. A pile had dropped during the storm last night, cascading down five storeys to cover the range, hearth and floor. I did not know where to start.

For dinner tonight we bought two penn'orth of chips and shared a portion of fish. The second bag of chips came free in exchange for a pile of newspapers. I feel embarrassed doing things like this, but everyone else does it. Mary in Pearks told me to go to the baker's in Regency Place, where they sell day-old cakes and buns for a 1d or ½d each. Perhaps Roland will wander down there one day. He is better at that sort of thing than me. I do save empty jam jars, which collect a ½d each in Lipton's. Later, when I went to spread the bread, even the margarine tasted of soot and had to be thrown away. That is our ration gone until the end of the week.

'Have faith,' the priest said tonight, blessing us both abundantly with one eye on me. 'It's your beacon in the night, the rock on which to stand, on which you must stand to make sense of it.'

Maybe and maybe. But meanwhile I can only thank God for the bag of coal and the bundle of wood for the fire, as the nights are still cold. We were without a light last night and had to sit by candle-light, as the gas-mantle had broken. They break so easily. I went to the ironmonger and bought a dozen candles for 10d. The gas-bracket in the bedroom has been painted over at some time and won't budge. In order to read at bedtime I have to use a single flickering candle, which can't be good for my eyes, but what else can one do?

It is probably me, but everything looks miserable, insufficient, dilapidated and austere. I have just suffered a miscarriage.

Emily Riggs cannot remember how long she has stood by the Blue India Light on the corner of Chadwick Street. She has stood there for as long as she can remember. And she cannot remember her age.

June 17th My sister Patricia came over for lunch yesterday. We had eggs, chips and corned beef. Pearks the grocers do a tasty corned beef which they sell by the slice. Whenever we have egg and chips I think of Phyllis, the cook at Woolland's in Knightsbridge where I used to work. Often, we only had a cake for lunch during that period leading up to the war. But if we took in an egg she would do us egg and chips, or save us some bread and dripping. We sat along wooden benches, always hungry but without much money to indulge our appetites. They were happy days in many respects. People got on with their lives in the best way they could. We would go about our work, threading ourselves through the seasons with a thread finer than any of those used in the garments.

It makes a change for Sally when Patricia calls, because she always makes a fuss of her. Patricia sells shoes in Lilley and Skinners in Sloane Square. Whenever we go there Sally pulls all the shoe boxes out from the shelves, leaving plenty to do, plus a frown from the manageress, when we leave. Sometimes we join Patricia on her teabreak in the ABC or Lyons' teashop opposite. I like Sloane Square with its fairylights twinkling in the trees. The area always has a gay and cosmopolitan air.

When I got home, Jean Farmer invited me in for a cup of tea. Her son goes to Buckingham Gate Central School, having passed his eleven-plus examination. She is very proud of him. We got into conversation about the lack of space. Her three rooms, which overlook the yard, are even smaller than ours.

'Of course, they weren't built for people with furniture,' she said. 'In those days people considered themselves lucky if they slept on a piece of matting on the floor, let alone possessed a chair or a table.' I thought afterwards that some poor devils around here probably still do.

'He's on earlies this week,' she told me, referring to her husband Charlie, who, like Jean herself, works on the London Underground. 'Prevents a collision, if you know what I mean.' Which I did. It seems to me that marriage in the tenement can only survive if worked in shifts.

The menfolk are rarely in evidence, except when gathering in silent groups to smoke and hang around the street-corners, like ghosts. Hardly speaking to one another, they appear buried in gloom. It is the women who keep the tenement moving by an internal support-system, reliance on 'tick', cleaning, visiting the pawnbroker's, and by taking in washing.

Jean Farmer proved a mine of information. Some here are so poor that it is not difficult to imagine a similar scene eighty years ago, with families living within walls of wretchedness: in rooms bare of furniture, and little more than sacks tied about their persons. Later, when Roland and I sat with our cups of Bournvita and our cream crackers, I repeated Jean's graphic accounts of Frederick Scullion, Violet Clixby, Wilfred Twaddle, June Flynn, Agnes Tillett, Cornelius Wilby, Emily Riggs, Willoughby Cleaver, Ernest and Gladys Playfoot from the market dairy, Bella Ricketts, Ruby

O'Keefe, Alice Underwood and Rose Sweeny. And not least, about her and her husband, whose marriage was not what it appeared.

Roland said I should write a book about them all for posterity.

June 25th We are five days into summer, which reflects the dust surrounding everything. I know it is easier with a baby and a pram to live on the ground floor, but our daylight is taken by the bombed-out Mission Hall of the Good Shepherd and the Victorian lodging houses opposite. Our rooms are sandwiched between street noises in the front and those from the yard behind. Then there are the night revellers, the drunks and down-and-outs, who seek refuge by climbing into the ruins from the back, or into the builders' merchants' premises next to it. Our weekend sleep is invariably disturbed by a variety of costers' brawls and the singalong-beer sessions, to the accompaniment of an upright piano.

Opposite   *Jean Farmer, who works on the London Underground. At work she wears black serge trousers and matching jacket.*

This unsolicited entertainment lasts from around 11 p.m. until about 4.30 a.m., when a Black Maria from Rochester Row Police Station screeches to a halt outside to cart most of them into custody for disturbance of the peace. These disturbances comprise frequent retching in the gutter, fights in doorways and arguments between themselves. If I were not so tired, the view of all this excitement from our bedroom window is better than any theatre seat in the front stalls, and more entertaining.

We never know who is about. There are strange post-midnight footsteps which walk along the stone passages some nights. Sometimes they walk quickly, and at others slowly, with a dragging sound. And there are those that stop suddenly, mid-step, like a ghost. Some nights I can't sleep with listening to them, wondering whose feet they are. Then Roland starts coughing again. When he can't sleep he goes and sits in the living room with one of his eight second-hand suitcases, stacked pyramid-style to form a chest of drawers. He goes through the smaller one on top, a soft leather attaché case, not unlike Mr Shell-Shock Victim, Willoughby Cleaver's. A case containing old letters, notes and thoughts, most of which are around a contemplative theme. I can hear him going through them, setting them out like parts of a jig-saw. No doubt wearing that faraway look in his eyes that indicates he wants to be left alone.

Despite the lack of space, we attempt to be tidy. There is always this need for order. And with it the need to impose order over things. So I tidy up as I go along.

I never get involved with Roland's work, because his painterly vision is different from mine. But I did glance in his notebook when he was out recently. There was a series of sketches: street-scenes and character studies whose immediacy of line forced them to live individually on their own terms. They were quite beautiful.

July 8th I have mislaid the fountain pen I use to write this diary. Charlie Farmer let me use his new ballpoint pen. They only came out last year at a cost of £1 14s 10d each. Charlie said his cost 5/6d. More like it fell off the back of some black-market cart! I suppose they will become commonplace in a few years. It doesn't give such a clear impression as a pen.

I have this obsession with throwing things away: old buttons, theatre programmes, a pre-war straw bag. All are attempts to clear a space. Darning Roland's socks; passing time to use time. Contemplating the ironing, yesterday's washing and the simple view of the wall. There is no escaping the mind with its dovetail into today. I wish Pearks had some Wensleydale cheese and I long for an orange.

July 23rd Sally is of an age where she is into everything. She has discovered the delights of the Army and Navy Stores Toy Department, which must resemble a fairyland of delights for her, wheeling the dolls' prams around and riding on the wooden rocking horses. My father, who is a cabinetmaker with a small business in Elizabeth Street, has made her a wooden doll's pram, chair and stool. The greengrocer gave me an empty apple box which I sanded down and transformed into a toy cot, complete with pillow, quilt and tiny sheet. She keeps her monkey, bear and dog in it. Toyshop windows in general are the main thing in Sally's world. Whenever we go out shopping, or for a walk, we have to make at least one visit to the Army and Navy Stores to observe some of its sundry delights.

We have the Cathedral and Westminster Abbey on Sundays and the Army and Navy Stores during the week to escape the wind, rain and fog. Perhaps no other building in London can boast such an enticing mixture of architectural styles, and who else will deliver a jar of Bovril to an outpost of the Empire, should one of their customers desire it? When I was a child I remember the main lift, which was large enough to house a dining room, being hauled up by a man with a rope. It has long since been replaced by four of the fastest lifts in London.

I particularly enjoy the Food Hall, with its smell of freshly roasting coffee and cheeses. The Perfumery on the ground floor reminds me of a Hollywood star's dressing room, with its multi-coloured glass counters, filled with bottles, caskets and vials of perfume, reflecting the sections a thousand times over like symmetrical patterns in a kaleidoscope. Talking of kaleidoscopes, Freddie made Sally one at night school from sections of wood, glass and a mirror. For the patterns he saved metallic sweet wrappings. He said he is halfway through hand-carving a farm set with individual cows and sheep, sheds and trees. During the day he is preparing for his chartered accountancy exams and says this offers light relief.

July 26th Roland's coughing is getting me down. He keeps talking about the 'doodle-bugs' and 'VS rockets', as though he still expects them to fall over London. There are those images of war which never entirely go. I wouldn't mind, but he allows Sally to play with his collection of wartime shrapnel. One has this feeling of being clothed in melancholy and unfulfilment as he sits beside his canvases, arranged face-side to the wall: a legacy for the spiders, rats and posterity. I told him he should forget his pride with regard to teaching and get himself a part-time job commensurate with his skills. At least he would be involved with some of the up-and-coming talent around, instead of exiling himself.

August 3rd Belinda, another of my sisters, came over last night with a bag of our old toys for Sally. I hadn't realised there were any survivors, but they had been stored in the loft. Then Dominic, Roland's younger and musically gifted brother, donated their ancient American teddy bear, Mr Putney: a family heirloom, named from their days living in that locality.

Sally took her first steps in the park this afternoon. St James's Park in the full thrust of summer. She simply struggled to her feet and walked off in a pair of red shoes. No matter how often this occurs, on how many occasions mothers observe this spontaneous act,

when it first happens to oneself, one is conscious of life's supreme miracle. I will always treasure those little red shoes. Happiness is a revelation that unfolds itself quite spontaneously. And now she won't stop. Shuffle-tap-stepping down the concrete passage behind me whenever I go to the sink.

I felt compelled to write:

Quiet, austere and composed
is Westminster at dawn.
A strangely constrasting hour
in which the air, harsh yet clear,
confirms its and our
individual aloneness.

We are all alone, every one of us, I thought, watching Sally enjoying walking, and playing with her new toys. But some of us feel more alone than others, isolated by the feeling that the cards are irrevocably stacked.

I can hear the collective mirth and talk from the women when I am in the loo, when I cross the yard or pass them *en route* to the shops. They have so little to be happy about. I almost envy their dogged ability to turn a blind eye, to eke out a living.

'We've a roof over our heads,' they say, 'and that is a lot more than some poor blighters.' And of course they are right. There is a stalwart quality and a persistence of purpose in these women; a deep-centred integrity of purpose in which they keep life ticking over amid this hundred-year-old, brick-upon-urban-brick pile.

The priest from St Ann's had the last word: 'It is in beauty we see God, but in silence that we hear Him.'

Opposite   *Many of the houses damaged during the Blitz are still boarded up.*

August 17th Today is the anniversary of the day I first met Roland ten years ago. A new lover is like a new life, a pledge eternally renewing itself. It is the sparkle in the champagne, the excitement in the caviare. But not these days. He kept a page from his diary – he used to keep one then – and I read it one day. I felt sad afterwards at how quickly the magical and new can become commonplace.

WINTER 1938

I met a lovely girl last night, Veronica. A name to enchant, as she did me. A saint's name and I hope she won't be. She promises spring in these worrying times, but today is winter. Katrina, Dominic, dear Papa, we are all starving. Veronica bought me a cup of tea and a cheese roll from the Putney Heath coffee stall. I ate it so fast I was almost sick. Such kind eyes and with the looks of Vivien Leigh.

Met V. again last night. I took her to the house to meet Mama and Papa. She brought a parcel of food. She must have sensed our predicament. Dominic naturally was delirious with happiness. There has been no news from Ida in Brighton for 10 days. No envelope containing the much-needed £1 notes.

We stood on Putney Bridge looking at the lights reflecting in the water. Lights lit by gas, thinking about the love I am beginning to feel. My life reflects in that water, spreading before me in chronological sequence. Leaving everything more splendid than I ever remembered it.

I took Sally and a bag of stale crusts to feed the ducks and to get some air in the Victoria Tower Gardens beside the Houses of Parliament, known colloquially as 'Boat's Park'. It is a long stretch of green with a few swings and a sandpit at the Lambeth Bridge end. There was a need to place myself beyond the reaches of memory and observe something of nature's quality, depth and substance, on less familiar ground. Whereas I often see the tenement mothers with their children in St James's Park, I have never seen them in here.

Dominic dropped in this evening looking pleased with himself. He had saved enough from his film-extraing to buy a set of drums and together with some friends will be playing a season at the Star and Garter Hotel, Putney Bridge. He usually sits drumming his fingers on the kitchen table when he comes, making Sally giggle with his way of playing the spoons. He cheers me up by saying that I still look like Vivien Leigh. He had a slice of my rubbed-in fruit cake and a cup of tea. We talked about those lean years leading up to the war when he, Roland and their parents often went hungry. They had lost everything some years previously in the American stock-market crash and had never recovered from it. They even had to borrow their boat fare home from Lord Northcliffe, who had been a family friend. Mr Putney, Sally's newly donated teddy bear, had travelled over with them, stowed in a trunk.

Mr Cornelius Wilby invited Sally and myself in for a cup of tea this afternoon. We had got into conversation in the Pearks' ration queue last Friday. His room is discreetly furnished and with taste, observing the shapes, textures and patterns merging in the semi-darkness. It is even less light than ours, facing the high, blackened wall of St Ann's Church. His room resembles a sanctuary with its dark-red velvet curtains and heavy oak furniture. There was a lighted candle standing in a Venetian red glass as if to indicate the Real Presence. He also suggested Roland might like to call on him one night, and join him over a glass of sherry. 'Tell him I've a good Madeira,' he said. 'And he might like to meet a friend of mine, Boris Pashkoff, currently residing in one of those service flats in the Artillery Mansions.'

Cornelius Wilby had also known Arthur Conan Doyle in his day, and Mr Pashkoff had done or been something or other in films. Roland would like that; he would have someone with whom to indulge in a few more of his fantasies. It would also be somewhere for him to go.

September 11th Our life, at least my life, is divided into days which transform into endless hours and weeks of washing, shopping, ironing and carrying pots, jugs, bowls and kettles to and from the communal tap. Shopping along routes of solitude, accompanied by an often, menacing depression about it all. For the sake of posterity, I made a list of a typical week in the tenement.

Monday This is washday at the local public baths, St Ann's, at the bottom of Old Pye Street, or bag-wash left outside the door for collection. Or depending on the amount, sheets, towels and linen can be wrapped in sheets of brown paper, string and a label, to be left at the Sunlight Laundry in Horseferry Road. The laundry is what I generally use. The rest I wash by hand, boiling the water on the gas stove.

Tuesday is my day for the library in Great Smith Street. On this occasion I select Richard Llewellyn's *How Green Was My Valley*, and *Sorrell and Son* by Warwick Deeping. I like this library. It offers a studious oasis of calm and I often sit in its reference section to write this diary. There is a good Children's Corner for Sally when she is older. If she sees me reading a lot it will encourage her curiosity about words and the reading habit. I heard an educationalist say that on the radio. I sit among local office workers and down-and-outs catching up on the day's events in the newspapers. This was the first public lending library in the country, so one can feel a sense of pride and history when using it.

Wednesday is the chimney-sweep's day, when required. Known affectionately as 'Old Nye', he used to sweep the chimneys of Belgravia when I was a child. He frequently appears in the *Westminster and Pimlico News* as a good-luck guest at some society wedding, kissing the bride. Now he comes to the tenement, where he

The library is a warm alternative to the Salvation Army.

'There goes old Wilby wearing his trilby,' is the cry. But he takes no notice, smiling pleasantries of recognition to those similar in kind. The mercurial dandy with a packet of sweets, a box of Swan Vesta matches and Peter Stuyvesant cigarettes in his pocket. You can see him occasionally loitering around Picadilly, St James's, or preening himself while sitting on a park bench waiting to meet a friend for tea at the Ritz, to exchange the view from the passage window for one in a more exultant milieu.

really has his work cut out. He arranges his broom and sticks on the floor, linking one stick to the broom end and each stick to the other, then inserts them one by one up the chimney. It takes about fifteen sticks to reach the top of the five-storey chimney, some 60–70 feet up. I, an obliging neighbour or a passer-by then checks in the street to see if the brush has cleared the chimney-stack. Although he uses a sack pegged to the range, there is always a throw-back of soot and grime, which takes days to clear.

A chimney needs to be swept at least once a year, otherwise a build-up of soot can catch fire: an experience not uncommon during the winter.

Wednesday also seems to be the callers' day. The gas-meter collector (sometimes leaving a small rebate), then the Relay Radio man for the 1/9d fortnightly hire-charge. Then I do the ironing, provided the Monday hand-wash is dry. I have to use a flat-iron warmed over the gas jets. A laborious and backbreaking process. The ironing board serves two purposes in this household: for ironing, and as Roland's washstand in the bedroom while I am using the tea-chest-cum-coal-bunker in the living-room corner, behind a screen.

Thursday This is the vinegar man's day for those in need of a 2d-a-pint refill. We gather around his horse-drawn cart with bottles and jars at the ready, while he draws the vinegar from a large wooden barrel with a tap.

Then there is the knife-cutter who sharpens my bread knife and dressmaking scissors. I have the devil's own job keeping Sally away from my sewing machine and scissors, for if she is not attempting to cut paper with the scissors she is playing with the machine's treddles.

Friday is coal-delivery day for those who can afford a bag. The coal also arrives by cart, pulled by four magnificent dray horses who deposit their own fertile comments in the yard. This is an exciting moment for the children and tenants alike, for whom coal is the chief source of heating. In they come, cantering through the main gates like an act from a visiting circus, with all the kids running and cheering in tow. Block after block, the coalmen unload the five hundredweight bags, carrying the sacks on their shoulders up the stairs and along the passages to deposit the coal with a rush in the coal cupboard and on the floor. Those without the means to buy coal in a particular week can be found foraging around for some lumps fallen from the sacks and the cart as it was delivered. The greatest fear is that the coal will run out before one's own block is visited. There can be a delay of several days before the next delivery.

During last year's severe winter, there were no deliveries for weeks as the coal trucks could not get through the snowdrifts. When it did eventually arrive, fighting broke out as the tenement men sought to jump the block queues in their haste to secure a bag, and to carry the sacks off by themselves.

Rations of butter, margarine, tea and sugar come from Pearks, the family grocers in Strutton Ground, where I am registered for the weekly chore of queuing. It seems to be nothing but queues wherever one goes. If I am lucky I will have a little change left from a 10/- note.

Saturday I do the shopping for bread and vegetables in Warwick Way. I walk down Rochester Row, past the police station, the Technical College, St Stephen's Church and the pawnbroker's, and cross by the pie-and-mash shop at the top end. I buy the bread from A. B. Hemmings, whose Victory Loaf lasts a few days. In the afternoons I have a nap before tea, the radio programme *In Town Tonight* and the *Saturday Night Theatre* presentation at 9.15. I prefer a mystery or a murder plot; something of Agatha Christie's, or a Paul Temple detective story with lots of suspense and tension. I do like Marjorie Westbury's voice. Sometimes the plays are so good I am afraid to go into the darkened bedroom afterwards for fear of something lurking under the bed. And they say it is only the artists and writers of this world who have imagination.

Some weeks the man from the Scripture Gift Mission calls with his booklets and little talks. How that man can jaw! I can hear him long before he reaches our door. He knows everyone's business. Sometimes, when I hear him coming, I turn the gas out, lock the door and pretend we are out.

If there is time, I prepare an apple pie, rub in a few rock cakes for the week, and then have a final cup of tea for the night.

Sunday is best-clothes day for the people around here and for the family dynasties in the lodging houses opposite. At least, it is for those happily in possession of a change of garments. Sally and Roland go off to Mass, either to St Ann's or to the Cathedral, depending which way the wind and mood blows them. Afterwards they often wander around Victoria Street, looking in the windows, or go sightseeing in Westminster Abbey, the Cloisters or Parliament Square. In summer Roland likes to visit a little garden near Lambeth Palace and follow the route alongside St Thomas's Hospital. I try to go easy with the milk because nothing is open should we run out. Some of the neighbours don coats over their aprons and purchase under-the-counter supplies in one of the council estate's shops near Page Street. But it's a long walk and I don't really want to get involved with things like that.

Sunday lunch is usually a shoulder of lamb or joint of beef, which, to my chagrin, gets picked over and left by both Sally and Roland, who are temperamental eaters. Depending on the hour we settle down to lunch, we often find ourselves serenaded with songs from the First World War. Mr Streetsinger, as Roland calls him, bellows forth in a terrifying basso profundo which shatters our ears. And then it is the tenement curfew time, the one obligatory quiet period of the week, which lasts from around 2.30 until 5 p.m. No ball games, pedlars, fighting, street-singing, or any

The weekly delivery of five hundredweight of coal.

Opposite   *The Scripture Gift Mission Man brings great
solace to the lonely and infirm. He seems to come every
other day . . .*

other form of distracting noise is allowed. And there are no exceptions to this ruling. When Bella Ricketts, the old newspaper woman, came home rolling drunk from the Grafton pub one Sunday afternoon, singing at the top of her voice, Mr Horace, the estate porter, was soon hustling her from the scene.

During the winter months, around 3.30 p.m., the muffin man calls, heralding his arrival with the ringing of a bell. He balances one basket on his head and carries the other on his arm. Roland likes muffins because they remind him of his nursery teas in childhood, so I often send him out for a half-dozen or so.

High tea comprises toast, celery (when in season), meat or fish pastes, jam and a cup of tea. We all listen to *Children's Hour* with Aunty Jo and Uncle David, followed by *Sunday Half-hour* of community hymn-singing on the Light. Then it is bathtime for Sally and a spoon of California Syrup of Figs. I use a large green enamel washtub filled with a jug and a kettleful of hot water, while I kneel on the floor.

But, intermittently, it is listening to the clock spanning the walls with time. Time I neither have enough of nor particularly want.

Sometimes if the weather is fine during the lighter evenings, Roland and I leave Sally with a neighbour and go for a walk around town, visiting Whitehall, Trafalgar Square, the Strand and Temple Gardens. The area south of Fleet Street is full of interesting courts and alleys. Strolling through the streets, smells, those powerful nasal props, those drain-slops and wet leaves in the gutter, present the mind with such an intimate register. Rich smells like Rose Sweeny's bubbling toffee and revolting ones like Bella Ricketts' twice-nightly trip to the loo with her slop-pail.

September 29th There is a chill in the air this evening, bringing the first hint of autumn's arrival, so I light a small fire. It is cosy sitting beside its light. It reminds me of when I was a child in the mews with Mother, Patricia, Claudine, Belinda, Freddie and little Poppy in her cot. On Saturdays we would wait for Father to bring home the housekeeping money, and after a slice of toast with Bear Brand Honey and a cup of tea, Mother would take us over to Tachbrook Street, a marketplace with stalls lit by naphtha lamps, where the bazaars with bare floorboards remained open late. Looking back, there appeared to be hundreds of stalls, selling anything from fresh fish, muffins, roast chestnuts, pink sarsaparilla to drink, to wool, crockery and greatcoats to wear. Some sold notepaper, others walnuts and peanuts, cockles and whelks. All to the enlivening sounds of barrel-organs, piano accordions and the gravel-based voices of the street-urchins flogging matches and bootlaces.

Saturday night market-shopping was always a hurried excitement as housewives, covered in shawls and carrying bags, battled with wicker baskets to buy the remaining wares, pennies, halfpennies and farthings being exchanged at a rate of knots.

'Buy, buy, buy your meat, Ma'am,' persuaded the punters, looking at joints of beef with an extra chop or sausage slapped on top. Meat has to be sold quickly or it goes bad.

How freely the mind can travel over these scenes. I wonder if today's images will unravel so distinctly? There was a poor old soul with a hare-lip who used to stand on the corner of Wilton Road selling 1d bunches of mint. I used to try to get mother to buy her mint even when she didn't want any, so the old lady would have at least one penny to take home. I often wonder how people like that ever made a living, so poor and patient in their afflictions.

It was a fascinating world before the war changed it. There was also a haberdasher's in Wilton Road, where mother bought rosebud trimmings for our frocks, together with lengths of elastic and ribbon. These were measured and wrapped in grey or brown paper, twisted into cones with the flap tucked in like a few ounces of sweets. I wish one could still get those flat, round rice cakes with tiny sugar lumps and a cherry on top.

I picked up my last issue of clothes coupons for myself and Sally. Dior's New Look has helped generate a demand for more variety in fashion.

*Chadwick Street, where the Westminster Teacher Training College
stands near the Labour Exchange.*

Opposite *A warm inviting world.*

November 20th It is now a year since I first came to view these rooms and they have not grown larger, no matter how often I rearrange the furniture. There are those occasions when the claustrophobia gets so bad I could scream. Moments when I could cheerfully open up the brickwork and climb through the mortar. Maybe it's the darkness, the fog or the feeling of permanence. I don't know. But what is certain is that there is nowhere to put anything and nowhere for us to go. We sit on top of each other and it is small wonder tempers get frayed.

I think I might take up Cornelius Wilby's suggestion. He wants to introduce me to his friend Mr Pashkoff in the Artillery Mansions as well. He says the floor housekeeper will make us a pot of tea. Anything for a change of view. Instead I rearranged the bottles on the dressing table and read for an hour in bed by candle-light. Being still sometimes allows one to inhabit some of those secret places time often misses.

> *To the right sleep*
> *To the left, life*
> *In this block sitting*
> *Lying within ourselves*

December 9th Roland has some film-work at last. *A Cage of Gold*, being made at Ealing Studios with Jean Simmons and David Farrar. So for a while he will be happy, living between takes on roll-ups and cups of sugared tea. The studios never seem short of things, judging by the range of cakes, pastries and sandwiches he brings home. During the breaks he sits and sketches the other bit-part players and film crew. Here and there a glimpse is captured of an actress or well-known actor; those quick, random observations and attitudes which so accurately register the mood and attention. The best are those casually drawn on empty cigarette packets, bus and cinema tickets. Dimensions suggested and contained by the precise use of line. We seem to be managing, taking each day as it comes. At least I am. Roland simply floats.

I have grown to love this section of Westminster with its contrasts offering vistas of elegance and permanence in a largely shattered milieu. Roland, too, has discovered the silent enclosure of Dean's Yard, whose unobtrusiveness, he declares, enters his soul like a much-loved poem.

Suddenly those anonymous shapes and shadows have transformed into people and I am coming to discover sad little lives. There are many who live alone, like Alice Underwood and Willoughby Cleaver, the shell-shock victim. Little, forgotten souls who will leave nothing behind to record their existence, except for my reference to them. My heart goes out to them as I wonder how they spend their days. Days without hope, money, comfort of kinship. Many nod in greeting, smile or bid us adieu while stopping to pat Sally on the head, for she has such wondrous red curls. But their tired, ashen faces, etched with lines of hardship, do little to camouflage their agony. Dark into dark and into further vacancy, they can never have known the emotion, how magnificent life can be.

My sister Claudine is counting the days to Christmas on Sally's advent calendar, because she is getting engaged then.

A GENEROSITY
OF SPIRIT

1949

January 8th It has not been a good start to the New Year, with old Mr Tyler from two doors down dying last night. He had not been well for months. A freezing fog was falling around us like a veil over his death, and our life too, in a way. Roland and I sat with him through the night, listening to his semi-conscious conversations with soldier-comrades and friends from his days in the First World War, who have already passed on. At 5 a.m. he hung up his years, and with a final grunt died.

I will miss him. He was a nice old chap with a long white beard. Always had time for a word or a smile for Sally. 'A child is a special person,' he would say. 'One of God's gifts and to be treasured, for they are only loaned to us. Take care of her. Make sure she comes to no harm.'

His wife died some years ago. There had not been any children. 'Met too late for that,' he explained. 'Better to meet the right one too late, than the wrong one too early!'

'The memory of one's own pain can speak most effectively when observing the pain of others,' said Roland later, no doubt caught up with thoughts of Katrina. There will always be a need for human attachment, but sometimes there can exist a need to view things beyond that. His dying left a stillness, reminding me of the Monsignor's words at our wedding. 'Always remember,' he said. 'Life is the most precious gift you have, and love the most you can give.' Life is certainly something none of us can take for granted.

> *For the moment*
> *There is no movement*
> *Nothing moving*
> *In or out*
>
> *Getting colder*
> *Shivering, damp*
> *Looking for things*
> *To burn in the grate*

All Roland wanted for tea tonight was a boiled egg. I left it on the table sitting in Sally's china rabbit egg-cup with the blue paws, and him to his own devices.

He never talks much about his day or communicates any of his anxieties. I told him how I had seen Ella Bonsor from G Block earlier, working on the stationery counter in the Army and Navy Stores; that Frederick Scullion found an old pair of shoes near Gorringes's staff entrance in Allington Street behind the Buckingham Palace Road. And that Ruby O'Keefe, whose daughters Janet and Susan attend a convent boarding school in Herefordshire, now serves in the ladies' Lingerie Department of Harvey Nichols. But he wasn't listening. What else is there to talk about when dawn points one towards another day? Seems only to prepare us for another beginning, especially when one's marriage has gone on for a bit.

February 4th

> *Mildew grey-brick and mud*
> *Shored-up walls*
> *Bomb sites with many a*
> *tiny yellowing flower*

The Grosvenor Estate has managed to rehouse Mother, Father, Freddie, Poppy and Patricia back in Ebury Mews East, as the flat in Lyall Mews was subsiding through damage. It is a poky flat, lit by gas and electricity, but Mother likes it. There is a climb of fifteen steps over a garage, with a smell of damp, oil and petrol wafting through the darkness. But there is a scullery, hot-water geyser, three small bedrooms, a sitting room, bathroom and lobby. Somewhere to hang their hats without bumping into one another.

A larger range of garments has now become coupon-free, so with the rise in the ready-to-wear market I might get a chance of more work. We have had clothes rationing since June 1941. The aims were, it was stated at the time, 'to control consumer spending and to release workers', such as myself, 'in the clothing industry for more important work making uniforms.' Which I did.

I see in the press that Princess Margaret is to tour France and Italy this year, taking in Naples, Capri, Rome, Florence, Venice and Paris. It will be the Grand Tour, once *de rigueur* for the well appointed. I wish I could go, but I would need a change of shoes. These ankle-strap, platform-heeled ones have a hole in the sole, so I wouldn't get very far.

March 1st We are in March again, our second one here. A pale sun catches my face through the window, which in turn reflects the image of the bombed Mission Hall of the Good Shepherd opposite. Of all the memories in my life it will be this vistaless view, this choreographed swelter of broken brick and torn-out windows, which will haunt me most. Sometimes when I see it silhouetted against the moonlight I can almost hear the

Mission sisters chanting and going about their tasks; or imagine the rows of people sitting in there for a service on Sunday evening. During the Blitz the hall took a direct hit. Joe Sugden and his wife used to go, along with others from the tenement, because it was somewhere to go on a cold night.

St James's Park today is covered in gold, lilac and cream crocuses amid seasonal tones of silver, ochre and lime. I have been growing a daffodil bulb for Sally, hidden in the bedroom cupboard.

Roland made us laugh last night with some of his quick caricatures of the neighbour-hood's dustier moments. Complete with captions, they illuminated tales of woe and comedy: lives lived without scenes; or scenarios to imbue this urban pocket of brick with colour.

Where I prefer the early dawn, Roland likes the evening hours. That uncertain hour between tea and dinner; the period of freedom, he says, between work and the nightly mooch around town, mingling with the locals, theatre-goers and tourists. A time to investigate old haunts, when he is not working at the Putney Regal,* to form connections and cultivate contacts. But does he, I wonder? I fancy these connections he tells me about are more in his mind than actual. Dominic has left the Star and Garter at Putney Bridge and is now touring Southern Ireland as musical director with a circus. Mother is certain Roland's family are descended from tinkers, as if to explain their inherited eccentricity.

*Roland eventually did get a job as doorman at the Putney Regal.

March 21st Clothes rationing has ended and Harold Wilson at the Board of Trade has announced that furniture rationing is also at an end. For most of us, the Utility range will suffice. I think of Misses Field and Oliver, and their 'Madam' gown shop in the Earl's Court Road, where I worked before the war. How happy they would be if this news could re-open their business. It was the implementation of clothes couponing which helped their business fold. People simply could not get enough coupons. I loved that job. There were about half a dozen of us in the workroom, busy with their made-to-measure clientele. There is never any elaborate work or embroidery around now to compete with the skill required then. I was paid £2 per week, which was a fortune. I would take an apple and a portion of cheese with me for lunch, and buy a crusty roll from the baker's a few doors along. And when they were in season I used to buy a large bag of Newton apples and share them with the girls. There was a nice atmosphere around.

I made up a thermos flask of tea for myself and a bottle of diluted National Health orange juice for Sally, collected the laundry from the Sunlight, and made for the Victoria Embankment Gardens again. Spring is here and I feel happy. Sally plays with her wooden bricks and skittles, and I sit reflecting over the passage of time, the cold, damp days of winter, and old Mr Tyler's china swan of coins, which he donated to Sally before he died. I had been touched by that.

'When my ship comes in,' he would say, 'we'll all go to the Ritz for tea.'

There is a generosity of spirit among the tenement inhabitants; help, advice, time and a sympathetic ear is given to whoever is in need. When I suffered the miscarriage, Jean Farmer was the first on the scene, ordering Roland out and taking charge of me, the evening meal and Sally, who remained under the watchful eye of her son Johnny.

It is still pleasant at 5 p.m., so instead of returning down Great Peter Street as usual, Sally and I made our way past the Houses of Parliament towards Whitehall and Trafalgar Square. I felt like doing something different, perhaps because it is spring. Roland was filming, so I did not have to rush home to cook a meal. There is only stew left, with cabbage. We can have that tomorrow.

Charing Cross Road, with its own brand of tumbling, late nineteenth-century tenements, bookshops and outfitters, makes for an interesting thoroughfare. Like Victoria Street, a few recently opened milk-bars are competing with the more traditional cafés and teashops. I browsed in a variety of bookshops in Cecil Court and bought an edition of Mrs Chesterton's *In Darkest London* and a copy of the *Rainbow Annual* for Sally.

Darkness had already fallen when we eventually arrived home, having enjoyed a bowl of tomato soup with mashed potato, and stewed prunes in a Leicester Square café. Roland and I should go out sometimes, do something before time catches up on us. He is fast becoming the artist who never paints, and the writer who never writes. It is almost as if he is already hanging on his own hook. Sitting in his own silence.

I found my first grey hair this morning. I'm twenty-nine.

Embankment Gardens, known locally as Boat's Park.

April 3rd The weeks pass in much the same routine: days of activity in which morning serves as a prelude to night. With spring and Easter on the agenda and with the quality of light, which is soft and muted, I continue with a growing sense of optimism.

'The painter Utrillo captured this light so perfectly,' Roland observed. 'London's light is something to do with the clay it is built on . . .'

Not to say its position in the northern hemisphere and its latitude. But I know what he means. London in the sunshine is one of the most beautiful places.

The couple in No. 62 have moved out and have been replaced by a lady civil servant and her fourteen-year-old son. He attends the Westminster City School and is learning, she says, to play the double bass. And don't we know it! Spoilt and arrogant, he is boo-boop-bedooping all night long, irrespective of its annoyance to others. It links with the scooters made from ball-bearings and planks of wood screeching over the tarmac, the smoking chimneys blocking off the ventilation and the kids fighting in the streets outside our window.

Although I am not Catholic, I like to sit in St Ann's in Old Pye Street sometimes. Its interior is very dark as one picks one's way through to genuflect before the Blessed Sacrament. Emily Riggs, the barrel-organ grinder, who is always draped in a long black shawl, is often in there too. She stands on the corner of Chadwick Street every Saturday morning grinding her old barrel-organ, like an image from a Dickens novel. In fact, many neighbourhood faces can be distinguished praying quietly in the gloom, revealing a deeper, more significant core to their otherwise humble existences.

April 19th I could have remained in bed all day, I felt so listless this morning. At times like this, in spite of spring, life leaves me with little appetite to take on the responsibilities of moving. What Roland terms as 'going out to untwist the day'.

Poor Roland. He is not of this world. Every neighbourhood dog knows him. He has only to walk down the street for one or another to bark and follow him. Eager perhaps for a sugar-cube or square of Bournville chocolate. He talks to them in the dogs' own language. There is always a special greeting for Rose Sweeny's black-and-white terrier, Prince, who spends most of his watchful hours guarding her trays of toffee-apples. Agnes Tillett, or Old Mother Stout-Guzzler, as Roland irreverently calls her, calls him the Pied Piper of Dogs.

I bought Sally a box of crayons from a stall in Warwick Way, plus a packet of Plasticine. Her delight in attempting images of colour on paper kept her concentrating for hours. She was so tired afterwards she resembled a bubble which was about to burst. While she was drawing I made an apple pie with cinnamon and cloves. A few of us are paying for gas cookers by weekly payment to the Gas-Light and Coke Company's showrooms in Horseferry Road. Apart from having only three burners, it is quick and economical, and when the oven is on provides warmth in the room. When the curtains are drawn against those outside intrusions, the place can be cosy, as Claudine had said.

If we had our own sink and lavatory, it would not be so bad. It is the lack of privacy, the continual flow of human traffic fetching and carrying water from the communal tap that gets me down most. But it is a roof over our heads, and many are not so lucky.

April 29th Everywhere I walk buildings remain shored up; cavities exist where previously buildings stood. I find myself walking with Sally in the pram a lot, just surveying the film-like scenes. The pram is useful when shopping and for keeping Sally out of mischief, although she is getting too big for it. I see lots of mothers around the streets walking those elegant bassinet perambulators. I see them in the parks, parked outside and just inside shops, or being rocked to ease a fractious child to sleep. Walking a pram is a bit like walking a dog; it can provide an excellent excuse to go for a walk by oneself without feeling self-conscious about it.

I borrowed an architectural book from the library detailing the era of 'Model Dwellings', of which this tenement was among the first built in central London. Built in 1861, they were part of a philanthropic move to house not, as is commonly believed, the poorest person, but the artisan in regular paid employment. Like the poor who lived in those dark and malodorous, mid-Victorian courts and alleys, our street-doors are so closely situated we can almost shake hands with our neighbours. I suppose a tenement like this, in its day, would have been a luxury, with running water, washhouses and internal water closets. At least they were considered an ideal way of housing the largest number in healthy conditions.

'We walk on floorboards paved in history,' as Roland said.

The umbrellas are up to interrupt a fall of April showers. Sheltering in the doorway of the Eel and Pie mash shop at the top end of Rochester Row, I saw Arthur and Kitty Melly making short work of a plate of pie, liquor and mash. Arthur waved when he spotted us through the misty glass.

'Here you are, darling,' he called. 'Come and try a nice fat juicy eel. Go down a treat with a spot of vinegar.'

My stomach shuddered at the thought of those slimy eels swimming around a tray in the window, awaiting the proprietor's knife. Sally and I shared a tuppeny ice-cream cornet from the stall in Tachbrook Street to take our minds off it. Sitting there red-faced and smiling, the Mellys reminded me of characters from a faded, well-fingered seaside postcard which called for a comic verse.

Lou Rigby, who has moved into old Mr Tyler's rooms, invited me in to show me her new bedspread and rug: gifts from her American serviceman boyfriend. 'He's handy for pairs of nylons, if you want any,' she said. She seemed a bit lonely, bereft of her family in these unfamiliar surroundings. She had a trio of lurid plastic ducks gathering speed up the fireplace wall.

May 10th I left Roland standing on the steps of the brown-and-cream block entrance, smoking a mixture of Woodbines and reconstituted roll-ups, watching the cloud formations. To the seasoned eye of an artist, beauty can exist even in the mundane. It was out of character for him to prop up the wall like that, but he was getting inspiration, he said, to the amusement of a group of mothers adopting similar stances nearby.

And I can never get the washing dry. Even though it is now May it still hangs damp for days. If it is not living beneath lines of continual drip-dripping wetness forming pools on the lino, it is wearing my hands raw scrubbing the garments in bowls of kettle-filled water. It is small wonder so many local kids look scruffy. 'With seven of us in two rooms, how can we keep clean?' remarked a voice in the queue in the butcher's last Friday.

This was not how we planned it. Our distempered room comprises a tea-chest (many of our neighbours have only a coal-bunker), covered by a board and cloth, to serve as both a cooking and washing surface, complete with soap-dish and bowl. A pile of ironing sits beneath a clothesline anchored across the room, which supports a wardrobe of garments without a home elsewhere. A domicile for a mother, husband and child. Our meagre possessions remain packed in heaps, between newspapers and cardboard boxes, like mummified remains. Guests' eyes travel with a curious motion over our living room barely larger than a cell.

Most of the rooms are worse, crammed with furniture, papers, objects best described as junk, their surfaces scattered with belongings. Many an inhabitant considers himself fortunate if he has a threadbare chair, a table and a mirror in rooms stale with tobacco, age, slop-pails and cooking odours. Every family has its slop-pail to avoid numerous visits to the WC, which is invariably engaged or out of use. They are a fact of tenement life, albeit a reasonably secret one.

However untidy some of the rooms might appear, given the number of items and people crammed into them, the yards and passageways are a different matter. These are kept immaculate. The duty porter sweeps the yard each morning and, one by one, the tenants take turns to sweep and scrub their portion of passageway. This ensures each section is done at least once a week. It was my turn today. Down on my knees, scrubbing the concrete, I was greeted with a motley mixture of odours creeping from the blocked rubbish chute. Ruby O'Keefe was doing her end at the same time. We shared a pot of tea afterwards. She is not a bad sort when one gets to know her.

Opposite *Lines of continual drip-dripping.*

May 29th With the days getting longer, I can see to do my sewing by the window. Hopscotch and other graffiti have appeared over the walls, cobblestones and tarmac again; with their thick lines and filled-in primary colours they do add a certain gaiety to the scene. It made me wonder where the coloured chalks came from, if not from one of those local primary school's craft-class tins. At least it is a quieter activity than listening each night to those deafening ball-bearing scooters. How they give me a headache. If the young hooligans, as I call them at times like this, are not hurling themselves around on them, they are hammering in a collection of metal bottle tops along the scooter's front panel. The kid with the biggest collection and assortment then becomes king for a day. They even knock on the doors asking for our 'empties' to take back to the local off-licence in order to secure the deposit and screw-tops.

Guests who call from time to time complain of having to dodge between circles of kids running and playing in the yard. Some find it an alarming prospect, especially if dressed more grandly than is the norm and thus becoming an instant object of ridicule: 'Look at 'er,' or 'Who does 'e thinks 'e is?' In time, their embarrassment and ours will prevent them calling at all. I tell myself I am not in this, that I am not really living here but am simply dreaming. That soon the dream will end and I can start all over again.

Roland feels that those of us who are neither writers nor artists are somehow veiled from the full thrust of life. That we fail to understand how they view the world and react to its harshness. I suppose he was implying that only those who are sensitive have the capacity to feel pain, can bear accurate witness to forceful reality. One does not have to be an artist to be sensitive, nor sensitive to be an artist. Either way, most of us can feel what is there. But tonight I am too tired for either argument or more nightmares.

June 18th There is much to-ing and fro-ing to get through the days. For peace and quiet I sit occasionally in Eaton Square with the pram. The railings have not been replaced yet, since they were removed for the Munitions during the war, so I do not need a resident's key. Anything for an hour or two of quiet. Mother joins me sometimes, bringing a bag of stale bread for the birds. Mostly she knits while I read. Either way it can be a pleasant change. I bring a bottle of water for Sally and a few home-made tea-cakes. She plays on the grass, picking daisies or chasing the birds. On the last occasion my youngest sister, Poppy, came along as a playmate for her. She and mother walked as far as Victoria Street with us and stopped for a cup of tea and bun in the Moo Cow Milk Bar beside the Underground Station. I left them around 5.30 to meet, head-on, the worst of the home-bound rush of office workers from Whitehall and Victoria Street. This evening rush is a sight to be seen and, if caught as we were, walking in the wrong direction, one is almost trampled underfoot.

We kept to the wall side, walking past Trueform Shoes, Dunn's the Tailor's and Hatter's, Kashieris's Restaurant, Rego Clothiers, Minty Furniture, Lewis's the Tobacconist's, the Victoria Shoe Repair, Burns and Oates Religious Publications, Macbeth Tailors, Hector Powe Ltd; the People's Refreshment Rooms, Costa's Café, R. H. Bath the Florist's, Leonard Lyle, Fuller's Cake Shop, Arthur Drew the Pawnbroker's, Connaught Mansions, Victoria Mansions, and Leslie Ling's Private Tours.

There is rabbit stew with potato tonight. The tea is finished in spite of trying to be careful with it, and that won't please Roland. I can make do with a cup of Bev Coffee and Chicory Essence, but he, fusspot, doesn't like coffee. He arrived home with a pair of black-market nylons for me last night: a luxury.

July 18th Willoughby Cleaver, the old shell-shock victim, knocked at the door today to borrow half a cup of sugar because he had run out. The poor soul; there is nothing of him. He lives alone, like so many around here, with little other than an iron bed, a chair, mirror, table and a blanket hanging from a nail in the corner. Apart from his tiny black attaché case, which he is never without, this is what makes up his whole world. How cold he must be in there.

'One doesn't require much to be happy,' he replied to my sad gaze. Maybe not, I thought, but could one describe him as happy? All I could see were the remains of stale bread, a few tea-leaves on the table, a broken jug and a teapot without a lid, constituting

his domestic crockery and provisions. I had an old bit of lace-netting I thought might do for his window to replace the shreds he had there. He was so grateful. 'I can live like a lord now,' he said.

Agnes Tillett from No. 63 said he had been some sort of foreign correspondent, having worked with such luminaries as Hannan Swaffer and Arthur Conan Doyle. Yet his life and room looked empty of reportage to me. I bought some bananas from Cooper's store in Knightsbridge. They are only available for babies on Green Ration Books at the moment, and I gave him one.

I have just noticed the date of my last diary entry: 18th June and today is 18th July. A whole month has passed with very little to show for it. Where does the time go?

I got into conversation with Ruby O'Keefe on Tuesday. She was looking very pale and tired. She was on her way to the clinic for a check-up, she said. It can't be easy keeping two daughters at boarding school on her own. There was a photograph of a balding, slightly sleazy-looking man on her mantelshelf, simply signed 'Uncle Charles'. I wonder who Uncle Charles is? I've only ever seen the priest in there.

'I want them to have a better start in life than I did. I had to walk three miles over muddy fields to school when I was a child in Ireland. I had no shoes or socks.'

Ruby's room was even darker than ours, with an odour of sleep hanging heavily around its crevices.

'I get very tired,' she said. 'My workload can be heavy.' I found myself warming to her and, in spite of her wan expression, with her auburn hair she must once have been what could be described as 'a looker'.

August 4th We heard tonight that Jean and Charlie Farmer are going to emigrate to Melbourne, Australia, on one of those assisted passages. Well, at least that is the plan for Jean and their son Johnny. There is a question-mark hanging over Charlie's future. Jean said the boat journey takes about six weeks, which will be a mini-cruise for them. It seems others have plans, or are seen to be planning their futures along other lines, while we drift. I will miss Jean; she has been a good neighbour. I will never forget her kindness the night I had the miscarriage.

Sally and I went to the park again, but sat on the grass verge on the other side of the lake. She was not happy about not having the swings and sandpit, but was soon playing with other children, drinking water from the fountain and chasing the birds. Over the lake, the snow-cream herons, ducks and geese swam between shafts of water, cubes of tossed bread and the sun. Within the quietness of the summer's day and the sky's blue warmth I was aware of the thinly disguised momentum with which time and nature fuse. At times like this it is easy to let in the happiness of things.

August 16th We all know their business, and they, alas, think they know ours. What they don't know, they invariably make up. A radio, raised voice, or simple moment of laughter can be heard echoing through the adjoining passages and walls. One can even hear a row going on some four floors up. Such is our lack of privacy.

But it is summer. We visited Green Park last night, walking towards a garland of blue–green trees under a pink–yellow sunlight. One could see through the shifting changes of the leaves and grass a scene filled with deckchairs and people. The band was playing within a circle of trees, offering a temporary respite from these austere times. My sadness for those tenement women, whose years of drudgery and hardship, largely supported by diets of sweet tea, chips, Spam and jam sandwiches, portions of potatoes, jellied eels and ale, have left them on a downhill path.

I experienced a brief happiness yesterday evening when we got back from the park. Roland spotted a suitcase left by the block entrance for the dustmen in the morning. So after it was dark he went and retrieved it. There has been a woman residing in one of the single rooms on the top floor who, rumour has it, is a stewardess on one of the liners. 'She only stores her belongings here,' Elsie Sumption told me. 'Been all over the place. The Caribbean, Egypt, Latin America. Brought me a doll back from Venezuela last time.' This suitcase must have been hers; it contained dresses, Bermuda shorts, scarves, bags, beads and blouses, all with foreign labels.

'Head Office ordered her out, when they discovered she wasn't living here. Said it was against the rules,' Elsie continued. 'Along with those which ban lodgers, dogs and usage other than residential.'

I felt like one of the small crowd that gathers under the Golden Arrow arch at Victoria Station each day with the humble doggedness of peasants waiting to cross a frontier. Who wait simply to watch the weary-looking, dishevelled foot-travellers coming through the barrier, carrying luggage and hailing porters. In the absence of one's own travel, anything second-hand, such as posters, photographs, films or anecdotes, can prove the next best thing. This morning I went around to Leslie Ling's travel bureau in Victoria Street and got a handful of pamphlets. At least one can dream.

September 1st With Roland in regular work, and me managing a couple of days each week doing alterations at 2/6d an hour in a small dress and linen shop in Warwick Way, we are still in a position to hire the Relay Radio at 1/9d fortnightly.

I go into the dress and linen shop every Tuesday and Friday, which averages between six and eight hours each week. Some weeks there is more work than others. It is a pleasant enough job, although I am in the basement storeroom with strip-lighting, an electric kettle for making tea, and a large kitchen table covered in American cloth. The machine has been electrified and takes half the time mine does. The shop girls from upstairs come down by turns to eat their packed lunches and make the tea. They sit at the table, read the paper or a woman's magazine, or talk to me. Mr Wakeman, the

Mrs Ruby Streetwalker, who teeters along at nightfall, in tight skirt, pink jumper, beret and rouged smoker's face, wearing six-inch-heeled shoes, towards Piccadilly to earn her rent.

manager, skips down the stairs at intervals like an energetic tap-dancer to replenish his stock or unpack new arrivals. My little cubicle is surrounded by bales of towels, sheets and linens, and rows of dresses, coats, skirts, jumpers, blouses, gloves, and boxes of price-tags. Mostly I take Sally, who sits quietly playing, but if it is raining I leave her with Mother or Jean Farmer for a few hours.

The evenings are starting to draw in. Dominic called tonight *en route* from a date at the Strand Lyons' Corner House, 'where,' he said 'apart from getting a decent meal, you can have your shoes shined, hair cut, make a telephone call, buy a newspaper or leave your coat at any hour of the night.' It sounds very cosmopolitan and unusual for London. He said he would take Sally there for a Knickerbocker Glory served by a Nippy. The nearest to all-night shopping I have been to is late-night at Victoria Station. That steam-filled gateway to the Continent, where the bleary-eyed can find a variety of late-opening bookstalls, fruit shops, cafés, booking offices and luggage depots.

I witnessed Mr Shell-Shock Victim again raiding the dustbins near Ambrosden Avenue. Whether he does it from need or habit I cannot decide. Either way it makes for a sad spectacle. Especially when he stomps off, findings in hand, to shout and wave his fists at the sky. How disturbed that poor man must be. Apart from the net curtaining, I must see if there is anything we can give him in the way of clothing and blankets, although we are a bit short ourselves.

September 15th The priest has given up on us, or so it would seem. Sally and Roland still go off to the Cathedral on Sunday mornings to attend Mass, light candles and offer prayers of both petition and thanksgiving; then etch watery crosses on their brows. It is a pleasant way of spending an early-autumn Sunday, with its evenness of air, peace, incense and theatre. But for me that is as far as it goes. There are a lot of Catholics around here, mostly of Irish extraction and who arrived at the turn of the century. The Irish woman upstairs, who lives with a coarse elderly Welshman, persists in doing all her ironing over our heads, by thumping down on a rug, which she lays over the floor. She uses a flat-iron heated on the range and the noise on our ceiling is deafening. It not only gives me a headache, but makes it impossibile to concentrate on anything else. When we complain she does it all the more. I wonder if she includes that aggravation among her Saturday-night confessions over at St Ann's? She only goes to Mass, she says, because she is Catholic and because it is somewhere warm of a Sunday to go when everything else is closed. How faithless are the apparently faithful, when one thinks about it?

Beaty Irish from two landings up, referred to as 'Old Irish', knocked at the door yesterday with a florin in her hand. She wanted to know if I would go around to the Italian-owned corner café in the market and get her a plate of egg, chips and beans. I refused politely and gave her something of ours, with a dish of currant pudding and custard. I was not going to get into anything like that.

I know most of the street-traders and market-costers by sight now, and am usually greeted with the odd wave, wolf-whistle, wink or smile, which lifts the time of day. Those anonymous pleasantries which also help telescope the hours.

September 30th It was announced this morning that a single person's weekly allowance for rations would be:

> Meat 1 lb (poor quality)
> Bacon 3 oz
> Cheese 2 oz
> Fats 9 oz
> Sugar 8 oz
> Milk 3 pts
> Chocolates and sweets 4 oz

Along with bread, vegetables, fish and milk, it is, the experts at the Ministry of Food say, a diet sufficiently balanced in nutrients to keep the nation fit. It doesn't seem a lot really, but with a little imagination, stretched with plenty of vegetables, one need not feel too hungry. When I do I nibble carrot and drink plenty of water. At least we won't get fat!

There is always someone or other attempting to kick in the door of the flat next to us. It seems to be an unsettled flat, judging by the number of times it has changed hands, ever since we have been here. But then, it is next to the dust-chute cellar, which in the summer, quite apart from rubbish fires, can be a little high. The flat currently houses a rough-looking woman from Cork, whose mouth oozes spittle every time she speaks. She and her old man and kids have some terrible punch-ups in there. Claudine brought over a large bag of cooking apples from her weekend at Bognor Regis with her fiancé, so I made next door and myself an apple pie. He is on the dole and she does early-morning cleaning in a Victoria Street office block. At least, she does when she is in a fit state to face the world. I have seen her skulking in doorways and sneaking out after dark in order to hide the latest black eye or puffy cheek. Their two children are left to roam around until all hours, while they drink in either the Elephant or the Grafton pub. If they are lucky, the children can be seen running around with slabs of bread and jam to eat. However, more often than not they appear to go hungry. Trixie, the youngest, has taken to Sally, often calling at the door to ask if she can take her out, or come in and play with her. She likes to get Sally's toys out and together they play with the little wooden pram and cot. I always send her off with a slice of home-made cake for herself and her sister.

Ruby O'Keefe locked herself out on Monday night, much to Mrs Streetwatcher's (Violet Clixby's) delight, for she had to hitch her pencil-line gabardine skirt up to her rear and climb through the bedroom window on the street side. The next day Rose Sweeny said she saw her entertain the parish priest for tea. The old devil!

'You should have seen the table,' I heard her telling Albert Mavrolean. 'There were tiny iced tea-cakes, jam-covered muffins arranged on paper doilies, like he were the Bishop!'

'To his way of thinking, he probably is,' was Albert's laconic reply. Albert Mavrolean was happy. He had just discovered that the Black and White Milk Bar near Victoria Underground had installed a game of bagatelle for its customers.

October 27th Roland has to be up by 5.30 a.m. for a cold-water wash-down and a cup of sweet tea, before taking the Underground to Hammersmith. Standing in smoke-filled carriages, coughing all the way to Uxbridge and Denham. I feel that to believe in illusion, as he does, makes for a perilous journey. A pretence world for which there is no eraser. He was a fireman yesterday, could be a soldier today, and probably nothing tomorrow.

He gets ten minutes to make up, wake up and slide into costume before the walk to Studio B. A reconstructed life on a reconstructed set in an old aircraft hangar completes the masquerade.

'Quiet on set, please', orders the director, as over and over again a take goes on celluloid, so fast in order to capture the fantasy-illusion. Assistant directors, crowd directors and crew; with sulphur arcs liable to over-heat surrounding them like guardians from Plato's *Republic*. Extras performing the light, the warm-hearted and memoried gesture.

The priest asked Roland what it was about acting that so appealed, as if to imply: why did he not get himself a proper job?

'It's the colour, texture,' Roland told him. 'Those flamboyant acts of pretence. The opportunity it affords for the escape from time, this tenement and myself.' And not unlike the priest's own role, I thought cynically; like the actor, he is also called upon to provide an elaborate floor show when occasion demands.

It makes me cross when I think of the money spent on those historical and glamorous sets, when so many, as Jean Farmer says, live without lino, adequate clothing or rugs on the floor. Or whose dire poverty forces them to walk hobnail-booted or barefooted over splintered floorboards and concrete passages.

Opposite *Rose Sweeny. Mrs Toffee-Apple Maker, supplies the tenement with a daily ration of sugar, tooth decay and vitamin C by the trayful.*

When I went to the dust-chute later some of the tenement kids were in the yard, obviously unknown to Mr Horace, drawing nourishment from the wind and rain. Their pale faces and agile limbs were darting around in the rain like effervescent cats. No doubt their parents were still boozing around by Perkins' Rents in the Elephant, Barley Mow or the Rose and Crown. A stranger around here gets directed not by way of street-names, but by the name of the nearest public house. And how it was raining.

Roland is still at Denham, working on his celluloid sketches, so I am left with the radio for company and some darning. Either way, his life and mine provide images which are coloured, folded and shaped to record and locate something of the tenement's duplicity and simplicity.

November 2nd Quite a few people moved in when we did two years ago. Those who, like us, had been bombed out or displaced by war. We recognised each other instantly, as if we were wearing some secret badge. Westminster people going about a late-autumn night in the best way we could. Depression can go, but the scars of a thousand pasts survive to contribute towards the fragility of the future. What of our sympathies, thoughts and longings? What of the aspirations which remain unspoken, are never given light? With traditional English reserve, we remain largely hidden from view.

In terms of films, Alexander Korda's *The Third Man*, starring Joseph Cotton and Orson Welles, has been the success of 1949. Roland and I decided to enjoy a rare night out in the West End, to celebrate our second anniversary of life in the tenement. The Bill Brandt-like, high-contrast black-and-white photography of Vienna and its sewers by night thrilled me so much we remained riveted through two performances. Harry Lime, the main character, was the original black-market trafficker in diluted penicillin, in the Four Power occupation in Vienna. Roland came away convinced that he too would become a star under Carol Reed's direction. Sally loves to dance around the room whenever Anton Kara's haunting zither theme comes on the radio, asking who the Third Man is and where are the first and second men?

After the film we went to the Lyons' Corner House in the Strand so I could see this all-night-opening, cosmopolitan café-restaurant that Dominic had elaborated on for me. We ordered coffee, rolls, potatoes and Spam fritters in the section called the Brasserie. Me in my couponed floral-patterned frock, amid buzzing conversations, the clutter of crockery, seats filled with Yanks in uniforms of tailored olive-green; and the ATS in their khaki equivalents and stockings to match. All our feet were tapping to the gypsy-sounding music. I felt quite drunk and terribly gay on a single glass of lemonade.

We were glad of the cold night air to restore our senses as we picked our way along a gaslit and virtually silent Whitehall. Not even the ghostly sound of a single bowler-hatted civil servant tapping his rolled umbrella on the tarmac invaded our senses.

November 15th It was difficult getting up this morning in the damp, dark and cold. I dislike having to put the incandescent light on in the early mornings to see what I am doing, especially when it is dark until nine o'clock. I could hear June Flynn setting off on her paper-round, poor kid with no stockings on her legs. Oh to live in a sunny and brighter climate. We spend so much of our lives living in a black tunnel in this country, with its endless days of wind, rain, heavy cloud and fog. When the sun does get through I have to protect my eyes from its glare with dark glasses.

'There she goes, Madam and her film-star looks,' I overheard Ella Bonsor remark. 'Who does she think she is, Lana Turner?' With auburn hair that is hardly likely, but, as Roland says, nothing lasts forever.

It was claimed on the wireless that the health of Britain has never been better, never more set for prosperity with full employment. With Government orange juice, cod liver oil, free school milk, they could be right. But evidence of earlier deprivation and malnutrition is still with us. One sees it in the elderly, bent almost double as a result of rickets and other food deficiencies. I see gnarled limbs, twisted fingers, swollen legs and crippled feet; bodies without an ounce of spare flesh on them.

Ruby O'Keefe's two daughters were home at the weekend from their convent boarding school. Both Janet and Susan are pretty girls with deep-set blue eyes, dark hair and with barely eleven months between their ages, which are six and seven. Their manners are impeccable and their accent excellent. Despite the adversity in their lives, they appeared modest and self-effacing, only too aware, I felt, of their mother's struggles to secure their education.

'We adore staying with Nana in Westminster Buildings,' Janet assured me.* 'She lets us read in bed by oil-lamp.'

'And bakes a fruit cake especially for us and saves us copies of *Sunny Stories*,' added Susan, 'which are full of stories of enchanted woods, red goblins and naughty schoolgirls.'

They made a great fuss of Sally, treating her like a little sister, which she, of course, loved. When she is older they could probably take her to the park.

*Nana – their grandmother, living nearby.

December 17th When I look around at these neighbourhood faces, I sometimes see behind their grim expressions a void. An inner emptiness they fill each day with chores, alcohol, distractions and gossip. Most of us, I think, live lives of quiet desperation.

Meanwhile, Christmas will soon be upon us, which means that I will need to plan a few things. We intend to spend Christmas here this year. Jean Farmer suggested I go with her to Lambeth Walk to get a tree, some vegetables and fruit, as they always have bargains, she says. This will be their last Christmas here. There is still some doubt over whether Charlie is going to Australia with them, but I don't like to ask.

Mother, Freddie and young Poppy will spend part of Boxing Day with us, as the Underground will be running on that day. St James's Park Station will be closed but Westminster will remain open, or so Charlie Farmer tells me. We will have a family tea and save a few presents from the tree. I am not sure what Belinda and Patricia are doing. Claudine will be in Bognor with her fiancé and plans to take Sally to see *Peter Pan* in the New Year at the Scala Theatre.

The Brasserie, Lyons' Corner House, the Strand. It offers excitement all night.

There exists a mystery flat down at the end of the passage. A mystery because it has been empty since before the war, although possessions and furniture remain intact. It is a two-roomed unit, shrouded in layers of dusty net and darkness. No one can remember who lived there, strange as that might seem in a community as familiar as this. The scene reminds me of Dickens's *Great Expectations*, where Miss Havisham's room, laid out with her wedding feast, remains untouched for years. One presumes the rent is still being paid, otherwise Mr Horace, the porter, would have emptied the rooms of their contents before now. 'It stinks of moth-balls and mildew,' said Agnes Tillett, who joined me on one occasion at the letter-box to peep through. We beheld in that light summer evening a Victorian world in miniature: gilt-edged mirrors, foliage, arrangements of dead flowers in glass caskets, and William Morris-inspired furnishings and fabrics. Objects which framed a lost inhabitance like a still life on a faded napkin. It was as though someone had walked out one day and forgotten to return.

Roland has been somewhat quiet of late, lost in that pretence world of his.

'There is a need to travel sometimes,' he said while drinking his tea this morning. 'There is a need to withdraw in order to examine and locate the path we are travelling on.'

I was about to utter some cynical remark when he knocked the tea-caddy over, scattering a million black leaves over the linoleum like a city of dislodged ants. Something on the lines that we were not travelling anywhere until he had scooped up those tea-leaves.

December 19th Sally is beside herself with the anticipation of Christmas. Janet and Susan O'Keefe explained the relevance of Christmas and the Nativity to her. Then Roland elaborated on Santa Claus, chimney pots and fireplaces. She has had an old sock placed near the little grate in her room for over a week now and can't believe that one morning she will actually find some goodies in it. I have told her that Santa Claus only fills those socks and stockings of children who have behaved themselves. So far she has lived up to that. Christmas aged two is wonderful.

We spent one afternoon making a Crib and Holy Family out of a Shredded Wheat box, pipe cleaners, cotton wool and an assortment of material scraps from my rag-bag. Roland joined in, painting the stable, a few trees, rocky ground and a Star shining in the East. We placed the model in Sally's room beside a lighted candle. It looked like a stage-set, ready and waiting for the director's cue.

The bomb site at the end of Strutton Ground is temporarily being used for Christmas stalls again. We bought two paper bells, a length of red, blue and green garland to hang across the room, and several packets of coloured gummed strips to make paperchains. What with the bargaining cries from the costers, the animated gossip from the punters and the accompanying French tunes from a busking piano-accordion player, the environment soon took on a festive air. The happiness of people who are loved and who love, are aware of things which money can't buy, shows in their faces, I thought.

Most of the shops in Strutton Ground have linked with the season by hanging tinsel and multi-coloured streamers and spraying mock snow around their windows. Together with the lights shining from the stalls, restaurants and cafés, they transported me back to childhood. I felt happy and warm inside, at least until I caught sight of poor old Mr Shell-Shock Victim, raiding the bins in the recess behind the Artillery Mansions and Grafton pub. Especially sad when, catching sight of me, he attempted to camouflage his action.

December 23rd An old friend of Roland's knocked at the door tonight, Toby Wentworth. He had been at prep. school with Roland and had linked with him at the studios in Denham. I was staggered to know that he knew we lived here, not to say a trifle embarrassed. He arrived in a shabby, double-breasted civvy-street suit, clutching a tin of chicken and a tiny box of soaps for me. With Christmas two days away, he was probably feeling lonely and in hope of an invitation. It was colder than usual, with patches of stars appearing between fast-moving clouds. Like my sister Claudine, Toby has that air of happiness about him, a radiance which makes one want to reach out and touch him. But his eyes, to my scrutiny, betrayed a deeper emotion. We had hung the streamers and placed the paper bells, which hung over the room in whispers of colours and transformed the gaslight.

I always liked Toby, although I was embarrassed by the unexpectedness of his visit. The room was, as usual, in a muddle. But I was glad to see him. Roland used to say Toby had a soft spot for me and, had I met him first, I might have returned the sentiment.

In spite of the piercing wind with its hint of snow, Victoria Street earlier had been thickly populated with last-minute shoppers. Those willing victims of the seasonal fray. I discussed it with Toby, together with the problem of not always knowing what to buy people when one's income is limited. For Roland I bought a tie from Austin Reed's while he was admiring the smoking jackets in the window of Morgan and Ball's on the corner of Thirleby Road and Ashley Place.

June Flynn goes through the White Arch as the council street-cleaning cart goes past. The sky is still a mixture of grey and mustard, casting a metallic glow over the macadam, reinforcing this sense of time and place. Artillery Row, Westminster Palace Gardens and Greycoat Place, stepping between Artillery Buildings, Spencer and Greencoat, pavements, dustbins and milk bottles towards the Black Arch which beckons her back to the tenement world. A stone's throw from reassembling and remembering, hanging her empty canvas bag back on the hook.

Opposite   *The mystery.*

Toby stayed until after 11 p.m. Roland was delighted to see him, taking the opportunity to reminisce over old times. And still a reserve in Toby. A reluctance to declare his present situation. It seemed he was lodging in a room off Winchester Street and researching a project in the British Museum Reading Room during the day. But that was all he would admit to. I, with my instinct, sensed something was wrong. I gave him a bowl of soup and a slice of mince pie and custard, which he ate with relish. Later, when Roland accompanied him to the block entrance, I heard him ask:

'Couldn't slip us a quid, could you old chap? See me over the holiday. Things are a bit tight at the moment. You know how it is.'

Poor Toby, poor Roland. Toby spent the evening sitting next to the fireguard, warming his hands above the flames. The guard was draped in an assortment of my underwear, a pair of Roland's socks and Sally's leggings which were airing for the morning. Poor me.

'Elsie Sumption was out in the yard again,' Roland remarked on his return. 'Bent over double, she was, like some Holmesian sleuth with a magnifying glass.'

I did not need to ask why Elsie Sumption was out in the yard in that attitude. A local character, her behaviour is legendary; she collects things, anything from rags, sticks, boxes, old papers to shoes and hats. Then she adds string, bits of paper, used envelopes, storing them under the bed, on the table, in cupboards, cardboard boxes, or on nails banged in the wall. Anything and everything; it is a collection to rival any aspiring rag-and-bone man's. She believes her collection might come in useful some rainy day, and after years of deprivation and hardship, her eccentricity is not uncommon. Many pairs of tenement eyes are glued to pavements, gutters, doorways and bomb sites in the hope of locating a local jackpot. I did not mention our stewardess's suitcase. Or the bits of lino, matting, the tea-chest with at least two pounds of loose tea left in it; or the chair, net curtaining and crockery that we have similarly retrieved.

The rag-and-bone man doesn't collect much in the way of joy around here when he calls.

December 31st It is the last day of the year. Tomorrow we will be in a new decade. The Fifties. We are Forties people, Roland and I. Are among those whose youth was lost to the Second World War. Whereas Sally will be a Sixties person; will arrive at her age of consent then. This will be a bridging decade, I think. A period in which to rebuild, re-cement the brickwork on firmer foundations.

I met Old Irish carrying home a jug of milk from the Playfoot Dairy. No doubt later tonight it will contain a couple of pints of Watney's Brown. And who can blame her? I don't suppose she has much cheer in her life.

Having completed work on Michael Balcon's *Passport to Pimlico* at Ealing, Roland is 'resting' again, as he terms it. The newspapers have reported a crisis in the British film industry, blaming the crippling entertainment tax and the devaluation of the pound.

He is out somewhere tonight, visiting old haunts such as the Colony in Soho and the Pheasantry in Chelsea with Toby and Dominic. For a laugh over Christmas, Dominic turned up in this New Edwardian Look, as the media term it, a look we see on some of the youth hanging around the street-corners. With its narrow trousers and bootlace tie, it is a change from the common, sinister-looking gangster-cum-spiv ensemble.

'It's the Teddy-Boy Look,' Dominic remarked with a grin. 'The face of the future: the Fifties.' I hope not.

I came to bed early and read for an hour by candlelight, hoping Roland will not disturb me when he eventually comes home. The Fifties, I repeated slowly to myself, as if to accept their certainty. The Fifties. It is silly to let the past with its disappointments creep before the present, like a clown at dawn carrying a bagful of prejudices and doubt.

'A Happy New Year,' I wished my reflection in the dressing-table mirror with my glass of water. 'No. There'll be no more clowns, if I can help it,' I told myself.

Mr Shell-Shock Victim, who stamps his feet and shakes his fists at the sky; who carries his world in a bashed-in attaché case and burns paper in the grate for warmth.

KIPPERS
FOR LUNCH

1950

January 7th I woke early this morning, aware of a mixture of emotions. Thinking about time and the beyond of time, war and the way it destroys. Thinking about the struggle for survival with its tentative, spiralling movement towards some moral certainty which makes life more bearable. The passage of time, I repeat to myself, is an unknown quantity. Listening to Jean Farmer walking with her customary swiftness.

St Matthew's Street at 7.30; dawn, with the barrow-wheels cracking over the frost-covered cobblestones, moving towards Strutton Ground market, where nearly everything is offered and where nearly everything finds a purchaser. The street-lights beam through pools of darkness like silk-worms on a length of satin. A policeman stands in the shadows, blowing his hands for warmth. A couple embrace in a doorway. I feel a pull, a tug to punctuate the easy darkness. I can hear my sister Patricia getting up beside sounds of shifting, above, next door and along the passage. She has been staying a few days to make a change from life in the mews. The floor has been washed, surfaces swept and dusted and the grate black-leaded. There are cocoa, bread, potatoes, margarine and herrings, with a little tea, cheese and condensed milk.

Florence Onions, the Flower Lady from G Block, has died in Westminster Hospital from double pneumonia. With an income that varied according to the season, she stood sometimes more than twelve hours a day for less than a shilling, exposed to the rain, sleet and fog. I am surprised she survived to her nineties, but it was her living. She had never done anything else.

'It's been a long day,' she once said, rubbing her bunions. 'I have to be over at the Garden to collect me flowers by half-past four in the morning. Then I have to make up the MPs' nosegays and the Gentry's buttonholes.'

Florence had been married to a former Leicester Square boot-black and had been widowed for years. Her son, George, still lives at home. I wonder whether he will take over her pitch outside the Mayflower Café in Warwick Way, trundling up there each morning like his mother did, with flower-baskets balanced on an old pram.

Patricia brought me my tea in bed. It makes a pleasant change to be waited on. She said we should take a charabanc one weekend to Bognor, where Claudine and her fiancé have a caravan. 'It's only 12/3d return from Victoria,' she said. But I doubt whether we could afford it. She sat on the bed sipping her tea, amazed, as was I, that Sally had not yet woken. 'She sleeps in these dark mornings, like a dormouse,' I said.

Mr Horace's daughter was starting work this morning as an assistant at Sainsbury's the grocer's, near the Metropole Cinema, Victoria. Kathleen is a rosy-cheeked girl with a pleasant disposition. She told me she would be earning up to £3 15s a week, rising from £4 to £5, plus the free supply of an overall and a good meal on the premises. It is a fair enough start for a young girl whose thoughts will turn to marriage and motherhood in a few years. I will pop in sometime to say hello and watch her slabbing up pounds of butter, and wire-cutting sections of cheese.

We were just about to make another pot of tea when Agnes Tillett knocked at the door with a collection for Florence Onions's funeral wreath.

'I'm just off up the Grounds and wondered if you wanted anything brought back?' I didn't but thanked her for her courtesy.

Roland plans to buy himself a new pair of shoes now he's resting. He said it was so long since he had a new pair, he finds himself dreaming about them at night. The night I met him he was wearing a pair of those black-and-white correspondent shoes. In fact I saw those shoes before I saw him!

'I'd like a separate pair for each calendar month!' he said. I know what he means, for there is something about owning smart shoes. They can make or mar an outfit. I would like a pair of black crocodile-skin shoes with matching handbag, a cerise scarf and a black pencil-line gabardine skirt, like Ruby O'Keefe has. We lead such contrasting lives. While Patricia and I were eating a meal of fishcakes, beans and mashed potato at the People's Refreshment Rooms in Victoria Street, Ruby was dining on seafood with 'Uncle Charles', at the Mirabelle in Curzon Street. It is all choice, this life. One can choose to do things that way, or this way. But maybe it is not as simple as that.

However, this evening Patricia and I tried out a Home Permanent on each other for a laugh. She had brightened her hair with Hiltone, transforming herself into an instant boudoir blonde. We both had a fit of the giggles, especially as mine looked like a wire brush. Fortunately when Roland came back its frizzier effects had quietened down.

Florence Onion's flower-stall, run by her son George.

February 25th The Home Permanent has softened into an attractive page-boy bob, which is popular at the moment. It makes such a difference not having to wind my hair up at night in curlers, which are agony to sleep in, and then unravel them each morning.

The Labour Party under Mr Attlee has won the General Election again, getting in by a majority of 315 to the Tories' 295 seats. There have been many rumblings about the continuous rationing and shortages of basic commodities, although some important policies have been implemented. Ever since the National Health Service became effective on 5th July 1948 queues have been forming for free dentures and spectacles. It is such a relief not having to worry about being ill and paying the doctor's bill. Although I fancy one or two around here might still be suspicious of the Service, not believing it *really* free. I did see the Hungarian, Elsa Petronovska, who is no longer in the active spring of life and who walks her two caged canaries around the tenement streets each night at dusk for an airing, actually seeing where she was going for once. Then Wilfred Twaddle, the Lamplighter-Biker, was seen in Woolworth's the other day trying on pair after pair of prescription spectacles. The counter was stacked with them. He peered down at a card with a large A at the top, ending with a row of letters so tiny even I couldn't see them.

One day when we are on the other side of this period, no doubt we will look back and see it as always being winter. As days with drip-dripping washing lines, having to dig ourselves out of snowdrifts and standing in ration queues. And it could be said that if we did have money, with so many commodities still on ration, there isn't much to spend it on anyway. But on the positive side, most of us are slim, have had to exercise great personal discipline and sacrifice, and are more appreciative of simple pleasures. Things like spare time, our leisure and the joy of having a banana for the first time since before the war. People collect gramophone records, go to the cinema twice a week, some go greyhound racing or take trips by motor cycle with their passenger in the side-car. Then there are the momentous occasions like seeing Leicester Square lit up again last April for the first time since the Black-out ended.

Very few women are wearing garments based on Dior's New Look of 1947, because of the continuing shortages of material and money. However, many women have learned how to devise ingenious garments from black-out materials, curtain net, butter muslin and parachute silk. Most of my undergarments are made from the latter. It has proved hard-wearing. My winter coat is wearing threadbare and needs replacing, but what with? There isn't enough money for a new coat, unless we go in for a hire-purchase arrangement. The women around here put items like their wedding rings in pawn for goods, or pay by weekly instalments to the tally-man when he calls. I lost my crystal beads in the pawn shop in Rochester Row this way. I could never collect the amount borrowed, plus interest, to get them out.

Mother came over in a state last night, tapping on the window from the street-side to let me know she was on her way round. It seems that my third sister, Belinda, is seeing a married man. Belinda is the secret one, with a special quality which sets her apart. I wanted to know how long this had been going on, who he was and how old. Did his wife know and did Belinda realise the implications of being involved in a triangular relationship?

'If her father finds out he'll throw her out,' Mother said. 'You know what he's like. It's his Presbyterian background.'

I have no experience of a ménage à trois myself, but as the eldest and the married sister I feel a responsibility towards her. She needs protection, if not support.

I stocked up on firewood today, carrying several bundles home from Littlewood's, the ironmonger's in Strutton Ground. Then George the Greengrocer saved me a few fruit boxes, offering to come and chop them up for me. He should be so lucky. Instead Roland went round after closing time to collect them and pass them through the window to me, so that the neighbours wouldn't see what we were doing. George also sent an orange box. Sanded down, with a length of curtain draped across, they make good bookcases or bedside cabinets. The magazines are full of hints like this. I keep my small collection of books, clock, candlestick and Roland's missal in it.

Mother brought me a bottle of Hall's Tonic Wine as I haven't been feeling well. She said it would buck me up. I had a glass at bedtime. It reminded me of communion wine and it certainly sent me to sleep.

'Shame about Alice "Lonely-Heart" Underwood.'
'They didn't find her for about a week. Same as William Holloway in
G Block.'
'Both died of the cold and loneliness, the porter said.'

Opposite *Visitors.*

March 15th The Labour Government continually urges us to sacrifice this and that; to work harder and produce more. I can't imagine what more they expect of us. Everything is spoken of in the light of austerity, shortages, queues and rationing, as a vision we fought the war for; one which does not appear to be materialising. It seems we are experiencing yet another overdose of Lent.

Roland came home tonight as white as a sheet. Apparently he had been walking around Upper Thames Street seeking out subject matter for his paintings when he had turned into Black Raven Alley. A fog had fallen, effectively darkening off an environment he felt to be haunted. Serves him right, I thought uncharitably, for wandering off like that in a dimly lit area.

I had a call this afternoon from Hilda Holloway, who lives in Artillery Buildings on the corner of Artillery Row and Greycoat Place, to see if I could shorten her elderly father's trousers. She hoped to hide a hole he had burnt in them with a cigarette. Close to Artillery Buildings are Spenser Buildings in Spenser Place. This small tenement belongs to the Army and Navy Stores and is situated next to the Greencoat pub with the Stores' Dispatching Bank for an outlook; it is the darkest place I have ever seen.

I gave myself a mud-pack this evening with a mixture of fuller's earth and lemon juice, spreading the paste over my face, neck and forehead. The chemist in Strutton Ground made me up a bottle of rosewater and witch-hazel to use as an astringent. My stand-bys to keep my skin soft are Pond's Vanishing Cream and Glymiel Jelly. After that I sat down to enjoy half an hour with Gert and Daisy and the Cheerful Chappie, Max Miller, on the Light Programme.

April 4th The last of the iron ranges were removed this week, taking with them a way of life. Block after block they went, with the men banging, smashing, before finally ripping the monsters out. This means an end to early-morning risings to black-lead and clean the grate. Although cumbersome and difficult to look after, one did get used to them and the surface was a useful place to store cooking pots. Provided one had the time to wait, the oven was a good place to bake jacket potatoes, warming the room with an appetising aroma at the same time.

Needless to say, at first Belinda did not want to discuss her friendship with Jim, the married man in question. We met on the suspension bridge in St James's Park for a talk, while Mr Hinton, the parkkeeper, fed Peter and Paul, the two pelicans, with fresh herrings. It seems she met him in the Antelope in Eaton Terrace, discovering how they shared a passion for jazz and a desire to eat spaghetti in a smoky Soho restaurant. Belinda, who at nineteen has never done anything so potentially exciting, jumped at the chance.

'He only had to look at me with those sad blue eyes,' she said.

'But he's married?'

'Yes, but unhappily.'

It seems they spent a lot of evenings together after that, strolling around Soho's more sleazy streets, redolent of Balzac and his prostitutes, having a drink here and a bite to eat there.

'The trouble was, we had nowhere to go. He couldn't come home with me to the mews, and he still lives with his wife, occupying a separate bedroom.' Belinda's expression radiated love and I felt deeply troubled. She displayed attitudes of misery and excitement, causing me to shiver as it reminded me of moments of similar anguish and longing. We walked for an hour, moving clockwise around the lake, with Belinda smoking and talking continuously. I listened, lost for words in my concern for my little sister. I wanted to warn her about the secret meetings, the nights when he would have to creep away, when she would try in vain to hide her jealousy. For there is not a woman who has been involved with a married man who has not lain awake at night wondering if he is with his wife. I wanted to tell her to get out while she could, while she was young enough. Advise her that there was no future in it, but I did not. Walking back through the blitzed ruins of Christchurch Gardens, we crossed Victoria Street and ordered two cups of tea in Costa's Café next to the Artillery Mansions.

'It isn't something one plans, is it?' she asked, miserably stirring the sugar in the tea. 'One doesn't choose to fall in love deliberately. It happens. One moment I wasn't in love and the next I was. Ten thirty on a cold November night, I fell down this precipice from which there is no obvious way up. And what's more, he's bald!'

May 20th Gradually items are coming off ration and this month dried fruit, milk and eggs joined the list. In a few years there will be so much of everything we will hardly recall this period of restriction.

They have made a good job restoring Grosvenor Gardens with lawns, flowerbeds and gravel paths. It is a pity they are not opening it to the public for the time being, as it represents a beautiful oasis of peace amid the ceaseless traffic going round it. I did sit on the wall for a time, feeding Sally, the birds and myself from a bag of granola biscuits Mother had given us. She is rationed with Mrs Roberts, the family grocer in Kinnerton Street. I sat and watched the diffident, the affable, the ready-to-talk exodusing from Victoria Station opposite. For some unknown reason I found myself thinking back to

Mr and Mrs Hart, our American neighbours in Ebury Mews, the night Belinda was born. How they had presented her with a tin of home-made cookies and a silver teething ring. Belinda who is now nineteen and heading for heartbreak. Thinking of Cecil the Chauffeur, Mr and Mrs Cooper-Black returning from India with trunk upon trunk of Empire goodies. And of Father in his office, attending to his accounts. We all have this need to be touched sometimes, to reaffirm that we are human, alive, loved.

In Palace Street I bumped into Mabel Wagstaffe with a party of tenement kids returning from the park. They had enjoyed a day in the sandpit and on the swings, having set off at ten with bottles of water, Tizer and one of Rose Sweeny's toffee-apples each. It must be the school holidays, I thought. 'It's swimming tomorrow,' said Mabel with a look of glee. 'We're off to St Ann's down the bottom of Old Pye Street.'

I bet Mr Lamplighter-Biker, Wilfred Twaddle, wouldn't mind joining her on the high-diving board, I thought with a smile. Mabel, who trained as a nurse during the early part of the war, has been accepted for Sir Gilbert Fleming's Emergency Training Scheme for potential teachers. She learned about it through a series of adverts in the newspapers. The way is open, she told me, because men and women are being selected on grounds of personality rather than on academic qualifications. I am delighted for her. She is still waiting to receive the date and place of training. Enid from the haberdasher's in Strutton Ground has been accepted for the one-year teacher-training course as well. Like my sister Patricia, she was in the ATS, and like the many other thousands of men and women accepted for the ETS, will be offering a wealth of experience in comparison with those whose lives have been spent in the educational system.

When I arrived home Roland was working on a portrait, using Sally's wax crayons. It makes me happy when I see him working because then he is absorbed in what he does best. It helps to ease some of his tension.

'The crayon knows what I want, listens with intelligence and obeys,' he said, quoting a line from one of Vincent Van Gogh's letters to his brother Theo. And I left him to it. We are going to have sausages, beans and mashed potato for tea, which I know will please him. If I were not here he would live on digestive biscuits, Shredded Wheat and cups of tea until the rations ran out. Then I suppose he would go without.

After tea I will clean the windows and put up the lighter-weight curtains for summer.

Mr Lamplighter-Biker, who cycles off before dusk each night with his cycle clips and lighting stick to ignite the local street-lamps.

June 3rd With the long evenings here, Sally likes to lean out of her bedroom window with her friend Trixie beside her on the sill. With drawing paper, crayons and coloured pencils, I can leave them safely drawing and scribbling until it is time for Sally to go to bed. Trixie has a talent for drawing little houses and trees, which Sally attempts to copy. About two and a half years older than Sally, Trixie attends the local Catholic school and already knows her times tables off by heart, and can phonetically sound out letters and words from the school's Beacon reading system. But Sally will grow up to be a dreamer like her father.

At eight o'clock the kids will be ordered out of the yard, called indoors or driven back into the streets, especially St Matthew's, which runs parallel to our window. A century ago it was called Duck Lane. It is a pity that ducks don't swim along it now. With darkness falling around ten, we have nearly two hours of screaming, running, fighting and various ball games to listen to. Small wonder I have a problem with concentration, the simple businesses of co-ordinating sentences, cutting out material or getting Sally to sleep.

> *Summer in Westminster:*
> *A tulip smiles in the*
> *Park,*
> *I wish it would for me.*

June 11th The quietness and afternoon light in St James's Park have a calming effect as I realise it is almost three years since we moved into the tenement. There seems little hope of any prospective change of scene for us. The *Westminster and Pimlico News* reports a list of over two thousand waiting for homes with the Westminster City Council, so any chance is out of the question.

Everywhere I look, couples are lying and sitting together in attitudes of courtship, confirming the season as late spring. Together with carpets of daisies and buttercups competing with the flowerbeds for colour.

From around 23rd July the annual Holidays at Home will begin a four-week programme arranged by the Westminster City Council's Mobile Entertainments Unit. Most of the local tenements and council estates, from Ebury Bridge to Page Street, Peabody Avenue to Abbey Orchard Street, will be visited. Complete with conjuring displays, Punch and Judy shows, acts of ventriloquism, amateur talent contests and fancy dress, even the bleakest of squares is transformed into an afternoon of pure charade and gaiety. Mothers and children from all round come to sit cross-legged on the gravel or along wooden benches. On the first Monday at 2 p.m. Abbey Orchard Street will be entertained by 'Clown George Moore', and the following Friday Old Pye Street will have Norman Major and Clarence Thorpe. And we are continuing to be entertained each Sunday by Mr Streetsinger.

I have finally got my summer frocks out from the trunk beneath Roland's pyramid of suitcases. Folded and smelling of mothballs, they will do another season. I have taken to wearing those canvas sling-back shoes, whitening them each night and leaving them on the window ledge until morning to dry. They look most effective when teamed with a row of white beads. Sally has a little pair with a bar-strap.

June 20th Roland has attempted to take up painting again after experimenting with yet more of Sally's wax crayons, liking their immediacy of effect. He took his easel, canvas, oils and a packed lunch to St James's Park, complaining later that he had not even the energy to mix the colours or to squeeze the paints from the tubes. I think he preferred to stretch out in the sun and sleep for a couple of hours. Neither of us ventures much beyond the framework of SW1, except for his nights at the Putney Regal.

I can hear Sally giggling from the next room. She is looking out of the window with Trixie, watching people like Bella Ricketts, the old Newspaper Woman, pass by. She bangs down the passage with her slop-pail as part of a twice-daily ritual. The stench is suffocating and lingers for hours. God, when I think what we have to put up with! The parish priest called on us one evening after she had emptied it down the WC. The whole passage and water-tap area was full of its bouquet. He probably thought it was us. I didn't know where to put my face. One can only imagine what Bella's insides must be like.

I feel Roland should seek the advice of a specialist. There is definitely something wrong. He shouldn't be getting so many headaches or dizzy spells.

I think I will pack a few sandwiches, a thermos of tea and a bottle of water for Sally and Trixie and spend tomorrow in the park. It looks like being another beautiful day and they can amuse themselves in the sandpit and on the swings, while I can knit or read.

June 28th St James's Park is Roland's park and Sally's. Both would live in it if they had the chance. It is part of a scene whose seasonal tones and hues are so subtly blended with layers of champagne, aubergine and chamois they take one's breath away. Roland says the park reveals something of nature controlled at its best, at its most forceful from every angle. All this in the fullness of urban Westminster.

'I'm not painting a picture so much as declaring my reaction to it,' he said of his work in hand. 'Not so much painting a picture as painting what I see.'

I know what he means. Painting is only effective if one has some knowledge beforehand of the thing to be painted. I had read in a book on English landscape that painters such as William Turner, RA, had said something similar. 'My job is to draw what I see,' said Turner. 'Not what I know is there.' It is only then, Roland says, that one can draw spontaneously upon and react to the stimulus around one. As with most things, one clearly needs a free mind to concentrate when painting. Perhaps this is Roland's problem. Why do those black periods arise, destroying his concentration?

Mr Streetsinger once trod the boards at Hackney Empire and the Chelsea Palace, among others. He appeared with the Crazy Gang, George Formby and others from the music-hall days, before his luck ran out. I saw him queuing in the off-licence for a bottle of Tizer and a small Watney's Pale Ale. Carrying the bottles in a paper carrier bag with a packet of five Weights.* Sometimes his singing is accompanied by a concertina or violin picking out tunes popular during the First World War; while on the corners the street bookies exchange bets and notes with men on their way home from the pub.

Star, News and Standard, Reynold's News, the *News Chronicle*, the *Daily Mirror* and the *Daily Herald* are among those papers and magazines sold by Bella Ricketts between feeds of bread and cheese, mugs of cocoa, plates of sausages and mash at her Victoria Street pitch. While she is munching away I have often seen her engrossed in *Radio Fun*, *Knockout* and the *Dandy* comics. Whereas people on our ground-floor landing come and go, somehow I think that we and Bella Ricketts are here to stay, at least for a time yet.

The four o'clock post brought a letter from Belinda. I haven't seen her since our walk around St James's Park. She wrote to say that Father, as expected, had ordered her to leave home. So she has left. She went first to a hostel near Barons Court and then into digs on the west side of Clapham Common.

'It's not so bad,' the letter ran in her spidery handwriting. 'I travel to Cedars Road on the 137 bus, walk along the south side of the Common and cross by its narrowest part. The air is wonderful. Some say it's on a level with Brighton so we get the same winds.'

For 17/6d per week she has a furnished bedsitting room with use of a small kitchenette. There are three other lodgers, two bachelors and a retired civil servant, a spinster who had worked for the Ministry of Food. Poor Belinda. I am sure she will be lonely, especially when the nights draw in and the married man fails to call on her.

I could hear the woman upstairs watering her geraniums, causing droplets of water to fall on my ledge. A sobering sound for a mind troubled. A mind consumed with my younger sister and her problems.

*Cigarettes.

July 6th The neighbours appear to be living out their lives within narrow kinship networks that come and go, while we remain. Families who have been here for generations suddenly seem to be spreading their wings with plans to emigrate or apply for jobs and homes in one of the new towns emerging. All we used to hear was:

'I was born here, my grandparents lived here.'

'We have lived here all our lives.'

'I wouldn't go anywhere else. All my mates are here.'

'We know everyone, share the same shops, schools, pub, loves and street-life. I couldn't imagine living anywhere else.'

Yet even as I write these voices are growing less distinct.

Their lives up to now have been based on a selected route which has been protected by an internal support-system. A route which, nevertheless, has been a breeding ground for quarrels and disputes, largely enforced by this high-density living. For example, there are nine black street-doors along our ground-floor landing, containing a total of twenty-eight persons including children and pets. Between us we share two cold-water taps, four water closets and one centrally positioned dust-chute, which attracts all the neighbour-hood flies in summer, soot in winter and fires at any time of the year.

'Quick, quick get the fire brigade, the chute's on fire . . . the chimney's alight.' And once again the street becomes ablaze with noise, confusion and consternation. When it happened to Old Irish recently, we learned that she had hidden her money up the chimney and had lost the lot.

Just now I did a quick count of the number of people housed in this one block. With five storeys and an additional room over the dust-chute on each of the upper floors, there are some 150–60 people, including children, living here. There are similar numbers in the other blocks.

Pearks have a larger variety of loose biscuits these days. Last week we had custard creams and this Lincoln and Empress mixed, with Mary weighing them out from large square tins. She is about to transfer to their branch in the Wilton Road, where there is a Home and Colonial Stores, Lipton's and a branch of John Greig's. When she goes and my yearly registration ends I think I will transfer to Webster's in Artillery Row for a change.

One only has to stand in the yard at night to see that every room is lit with inhabited life. I take a deep breath and breathe out slowly in order not to feel as though I am suffocating. Then I listen to the feet again, the feet which tramp up and down the passages. Sounds which are familiar, almost reassuring with their persistence.

August 2nd I woke this morning in a bad mood. It wasn't any one thing in particular, simply an accumulation of things. I spent most of yesterday evening boiling together old stockings in a large saucepan to blend the colour, and darning them. Make Do and Mend is all I ever do, dyeing scuffed shoes, darning old socks and unpicking worn frocks to resurrect into a change of garment. It was a hot and airless night, with my lying awake for most of it. I got up at 5.30, leaving Roland snoring beneath the blankets.

Resentment for lost opportunities can be a very easy emotion, forcing one to question the validity of things: our life and place in it. Sentiment which can leave us feeling more desperate and alone. Times when the trees in the parks press closer together and the grass creeps up to form corners. When even the fragrance of the flowers, the beauty and gaiety of the sun playing on the water, those views 'set in the brushstrokes of an aspiring Matisse', as Roland refers to them, can't come in to help me. Times heightened by my own fragility and inconsequence before Sally comes running over again, and I am transported and reassured of things. Reassured of life, my life in Sally's and hers in the world. The miracle of life. It must be like death not to have children of one's own.

The silence around Belinda worries me. She never answered my letter posted to an address in Percy Street W1, where her married man friend is now living with her, opting for the Fitzrovia cognoscenti. A girl I worked with at Woolland's had lodged in Charlotte Street, cycling in to work each day from Tottenham Court Road. She said that, in spite of wartime shortages, a plate of spaghetti and grated cheese could always be had in one of the cafés. Dominic knows the area, playing in some of the clubs, accompanying a concertina and mandoline for members of London's bohemia. 'It's London's *Quartier Latin*,' he told me, 'complete with studios, narrow streets full of pubs and continental foodshops. The black market operates well here. Roland would love the place.'

It seems as though some of Roland's old art crowd hang out there too. Artists like Walter Sickert, Rex Whistler and Duncan Grant, who frequented and lived in the area in the Thirties, set much of its tone. And those around today live a little like we do, from hand to mouth.

'They sit around tables with red cloths, smoking and drinking coffee, talking about art, writing, discussing who's publishing what, who's selling their paintings and where they are exhibiting, with witty exchanges and anecdotes,' Roland said. I think Dominic should invite him to go with him on one of his gigs next time.

*Bella Ricketts is not liked. No one speaks to her and
everyone avoids her if they can. She knows that. It's the
smell from her pail as she thumps along the passage with it.
'It's disgusting. Shouldn't be allowed.'
'What is this place coming to?'
'God. What we have to put up with.'*

August 10th A group of women were clustered around a spiv in Strutton Ground market at lunchtime. I nearly bought a pair of nylons, but decided against it. Had I discovered a run in them when I got home, I wouldn't be able to change them or get my money back. These men are here today and gone tomorrow. 'Every one perfect,' he cried. 'Only half a quid a pair.'

And meanwhile Kathy down the passage consults her horoscope to give her days a perimeter which otherwise might not exist. And Lita, next door to Ruby O'Keefe, looks set to emulate her by going out at night dressed like a human neon sign with all the goods on show. I have to laugh to myself. We certainly have a variety of neighbours. One concludes Lita has more than enough to pay her weekly rent now.

I took Frederick Scullion a small Hovis loaf, some cheese and a small tin of cocoa as I overheard he had been ill. He was as white as a sheet, sitting by the window in an old wooden chair. I simply knocked on the door, hesitated until I heard his voice, and let myself in, as is the habit around here. He looked touched by my gesture, making me wish I could have given him more. Elsie Sumption and Agnes Tillett had looked in earlier, one with a rag rug to cover his knees and the other with a packet of sandwiches and two warm jacket potatoes wrapped in a cloth.

'The women around here don't get much,' he told me. 'Their men take most of it for beer, skittles and tobacco. And what's left of that they blow on the dogs.'

I could make out the curved definition of a chamber pot amid the gloom under his iron single bed, confirming once again our basic lack of amenities and privacy.

'I hear them talking in the queue in Kennedy's,' he went on. 'I've no idea what he gets, they say, only what he gives me. I can't imagine your husband being like that. He's a gentleman.'

September 17th A visitor to the tenement can observe at a glance that it is mostly women around here: wives, mothers, sisters and maiden aunts, with widows and children. Their men are abroad serving with the forces. As with us, money is scarce, allowing them few home comforts. Extra money is brought in from office cleaning, washing, stall-holding in the market, or by baby-minding. Their lot is not a happy one, living mostly with an absent husband, and centring their lives around their children and hearth. The men who are here never seem to be around for comfort or affection, except the Friday late-night ritual of board and bed, with a bonus thrown in after the Sunday lunch of roast beef and Yorkshire pudding. We are lucky in comparison, I think, sometimes.

Bella Ricketts, the old Newspaper Woman of slop-pail fame, lives alone in one room with a bed in the corner, a table, jug and bowl which is kept behind a curtain. There is generally a large iron pot, which some refer to as her 'cauldron', in evidence, with some evil-smelling gruel stewing in it. The place is always in a mess, but then no one cares. She never has any callers except the Scripture Gift Mission man, who invariably gets a barrage of abuse; and some say she has seen three husbands off in their prime. And rumour has it she is still stewing the remains of their bones in her pot. Apart from the smell and the muttering to herself which goes on for hours behind the stone walls, most seem oblivious of her existence. No one here seeks to rupture the membrane which separates this world from the one outside.

It always seems to be raining, no matter which season, with its drip-dripping wetness over the asphalt. Dirty dishes, empty beer bottles, cigarette ends amid old newspapers lying around the floor, are a commonplace sight. And no one appears ever to make their beds. No one aspires to have more than their neighbours in the way of material possessions. Nor seeks to go beyond the immediate environment, or to move away. So content, they appear locked and interwoven into the fabric of their restricted kinships and groups. If one is seen to be aloof, reserved, or in any way different from the norm, one is held as an object of suspicion.

'You're not like us,' they say. And indeed we are not.

Thinking in horizontal lines, so to speak, provides me with an escape, a way of casting

Frederick Scullion is at the far end of the corridor — a black door which opens on to a tiny cell-like room comprising his life, world and belongings. Not much to account for his seventy-seven years.

around for fresh mental images and excursions into colour, regardless of the chores I am engaged upon. Thinking about Mr Pashkoff in the Artillery Mansions with his black-market Russian tea and box of Turkish Delight; and Cornelius Wilby's recent visit to a friend in Rossetti Mansions in Chelsea, where he was given an original 1918 scrapbook detailing the unexpected arrival in London of Diaghilev's Russian Ballet. The dear old man had been beside himself with excitement.

'This is a Collector's Item,' he said. 'Look, see here. Pictures of their new stars, Lydia Lopokova and Massine at the Coliseum, lunching at the Tour Eiffel Restaurant and Café Royale, where Bloomsbury were in force.' By Bloomsbury he meant Duncan Grant, Lytton Strachey, Carrington, the Sitwells and Augustus John. Roland shared his excitement, insisting he join us for dinner, which comprised spring greens and toad-in-the-hole. Cornelius orchestrated the warm summer evening, reciting lines from T. S. Eliot's *The Waste Land*, and engaging Roland in a discussion about the mediaeval quests of Arthurian legend that underlie it. Roland seemed to be temporarily transported, especially when combined with anecdotes of conversations Cornelius once held with Noël Coward.

Retiring later, my mood has moved on a bit, proving how important it is to share time with friends occasionally.

September 23rd My sister Patricia came for tea today, bringing a quarter-pound bag of peppermints for Sally, who immediately insisted on calling them 'pumpermints', and a box of madeleine cakes for me. Roland had a pair of cut-price slippers, which I know he will never wear, declaring them items *gentlemen* have no use for. There are things from his background he will hold until the grave, those attempts at maintaining a certain dignity and gravity of manner. I made the tea while Patricia laid the table with her usual happy smile. She has moved out of the flat in Ebury Mews and found herself an attic bedsitting-room off Putney High Street.

My sisters seem to be spreading their wings, and with Freddie doing National Service it leaves just Poppy at home, experimenting with a range of cosmetics from Boots, Woolworth's and Peter Jones, Sloane Square. She avidly follows the 'instant beauty' guidelines in women's magazines such as *My Home* and *Woman*, with a touch of rouge, lipstick, Angel Face powder and Astral cream. She draws an eyebrow-pencil seam up the back of her powdered legs as make-believe nylon stockings. Poppy, who is more creatively inclined than academic, is the only one among us affected by the raising of the school leaving age to fifteen on 1st April 1947.

'It's a waste of a year,' she protested at the time. 'I could be out earning money instead of sitting in a makeshift classroom writing essays on the way we see Britain moving in the late nineteen fifties, baking rock cakes or finding ways to play truant.'

The desire to continue her education may come later. One's adolescent years can be disturbing, with their contrasting periods of introspection, vulnerability, self-consciousness and restlessness. Claudine and Freddie were 'scholarship kids', as those passing their eleven-plus to the grammar school became known, and left at ages sixteen and seventeen respectively.

Patricia was looking very pretty, wearing her hair tied back in a ponytail, and a pair of black patent pumps. She had me giggling with her colourful mimicry of Max Miller's *Blue Book of Jokes*. She had seen him on stage at the Chelsea Palace Music Hall in the King's Road.

After a meal comprising an omelette made with dried-egg powder, and a slice of cold apple tart, we walked in the rain to the bus stop with Sally holding hands between us. A happy child. Patricia caught the No. 11 for Sloane Square where the No. 22 will take her on to Putney. Standing by the Army and Navy Stores I noticed their clock was ten minutes slow. I wondered how many were late for work this morning because of that. The bus arrived amid a glitter of raindrops, with umbrellas and plastic rain macs reflecting what little remained of the light. The bus was more crowded than usual, with three already standing, and had a smell of damp clothes. The conductor let Patricia and one man on. No one got off, so I imagine most were bound for Victoria Station although it was past rush-hour.

I think Patricia is lonely living on her own like that. She fell out with Father over something or other and he threw her out. It can happen in the best of families during that

difficult transition between dependence and independence. She is highly strung and volatile, even worse than me. A lot of her troubles began during those early war years when she, Belinda and Freddie were evacuated. She thought she was never coming home and the people she stayed with were not particularly kind. So many hidden insecurities will have been formed through that exercise, when one thinks of all those tiny children wrenched from their families for an indefinite period. I feel sure it will come out one day, the way it may have affected their relationships in later life.

Sally announced that Patricia is her favourite aunt. They are alike in both temperament and looks. I will clear away the dishes, fill the kettle for the morning and have an early night. Roland is out with Toby and Dominic somewhere, which I am happy about. He needs their company, to share useful exchanges of ideas. So long as he doesn't disturb me when he comes in.

September 28th To think that Victoria Street, with its shopping and office workers bound for the station each night, barely existed a century ago. Where the links of the then new buildings had not yet joined, one could see the fag-ends of the courts and interiors of the ruined houses which marked the perimeter of the tenement, so a writer of the period described. Where refuse ran out like black streams. So amiable, familiar, as tuned in to life its inhabitants retreat into darkness, captivity and escape.

Sheer strength of character is what predominates around here: with its unselfishness, consideration, humbleness, with the odd exception, and gentle human kindness. When I think of Alice Underwood forsaking her usual plate of salt-and-vinegar chips to give me one bearing beetroot and slices of bread one day when I was particularly short of money. Or Cyril Pearce gathering up a variety of litter, which reflects our assorted tastes, habits and lapses, with such quiet dignity. His is a humble occupation, but one, nevertheless, carried out tidily dressed in a thin coat and broken-down shoes as he sweeps up a few shillings for himself. And Mr Merriweather, the police constable, pacing the streets, peering into doorways to assure himself of their emptiness; checking over streets that are not quite dark, but in an atmosphere of darkness. When Tommy Hooper, the night-watchman, who tells me he doesn't watch all night, begins to stoke his coke fire as the clocks strike.

In the surrounding streets, which are quiet but not silent, a lorry loading the morning milk-churns starts up; then the street-cleaner steams into action amid buildings which rustle, creak and rattle like unspoken ghosts at this hour. When the postman, about to embark upon his first delivery, senses the vulnerability of life, when his and everyone else's silhouettes achieve perfect harmony with the sweeping lines of the streets. Each image noting the definiteness of human agency. Especially when the buses begin to crawl down Victoria Street like a funeral cortège.

The bus stop in Victoria Street.

Roland has just come in with a packet of soda mints, a septic pencil and aspirin obtained in Lyons' Corner House's automatic machine. Something to do with the novelty of pushing the correct buttons and pulling open the drawer, he said. I went to bed opening the curtains for the morning. Emile Zola once wrote that London's beauty lies in its immensity. Westminster's, surely, must lie in its anonymity.

October 1st We keep trying the Council and the Grosvenor Estate to get on their waiting lists, but they insist we are adequately housed. Adequately! With no sink, kitchen, running water, WC or bath. Roland says life is simply God, poetry, art, soul and death. It might exemplify his vision but it doesn't mine, when consumed with this heroic, day-to-day struggle for survival. What with the creaking stairs, odours of rotting food, over-cooked cabbage, mouldy walls, peeling distemper and general, loitering wretchedness, it is not difficult to look back, as I frequently do, to this area when Cardinal Wiseman* spoke of its holes and corners of congealed wretchedness about the Abbey. He was one of the first to popularise the word 'slum'. This area was one of the original sinks of iniquity and vice, known as the Almonry. When I find myself in this mood my thoughts turn to Jeremy, now married to a landowner's daughter. The wedding at St Margaret's, Westminster, was reviewed last month in the *Tatler* and announced in the personal columns of *The Times*. They will never know a life other than one in which privilege, position and wealth is taken for granted. When I read about it in the library, my heart missed a beat, leaving me unsettled for days afterwards.

An old man who lives on the top floor was taken ill in the week. Agnes Tillett summoned me to go with her, not wanting to enter alone. He was lying in the middle of a large double bed so jammed in all round it could barely accommodate the chest of drawers, washstand and dressing table. His eyes were drawn, skin flabby and matching the set of false teeth yellowing in an aluminium container. His exposed neck revealed folds of skin over his windpipe. Agnes Tillett attempted to feed him with some porridge while I looked around for some method of making tea. The frail old man should not be living at the top of four flights of stairs. How he manages to get up them I will never know, but he does. They all do, others in similar plights. Plod, plod, pace after pace, climbing each stone step in between gasps of breath. I located the tea-caddy alongside a moulding kipper, a postcard with views of Ramsgate, Hayling Island and Clifton Sands, and an edition of *Reynold's News* in the sideboard drawer. His was a case of personal neglect, I think, brought on by a mixture of age, malnutrition, poverty and loneliness. The good to come from this is that he now has two more friends to keep an eye on him.

The tea, with a few arrowroot biscuits, seemed to revive him. I ran down to Goodall's, the corner shop in Old Pye Street, to get him one or two other basic items. I then left him in the capable hands of Agnes Tillett and Elsie Sumption, who had joined us.

*Cardinal Archbishop of Westminster in 1850.

I was in the middle of Drummer dyeing some clothes. To maintain an even colour one has to keep the garment continually moving in the vat of simmering water. I dyed a few items last week using my favourite black again. It works more successfully than other colours, especially with lengths of lace and velvet ribbon applied afterwards to give a tired outfit a new lease of life.

The evenings are drawing in again with their seasonal chill; time to haul on our overcoats and sit draped in shawls. I took the tram from Victoria along Vauxhall Bridge Road as far as Moreton Street to visit the WVS Clothing Exchange. The tram passed by some of the many new prefabricated homes being erected in the district. Liza Kinsman, who was bombed out from Bennett's Yard near Marsham Street, has one. She said many come complete with electric cooker, refrigerator and an electric water-heater. With their little gardens and self-contained measure of privacy, I wouldn't say no to one. There are a few near the fish-and-chip shop in Regency Street.

October 22nd The four o'clock post brought a letter postmarked Brighton for Roland. It contained the news that his octogenarian Aunt Ida was dying. I emptied old Mr Tyler's china swan and a tin of Sally's threepenny bits and we went by charabanc from Victoria Coastal Chambers this afternoon. I packed a thermos of tea, a packet of cheese-and-tomato sandwiches and left Sally with Trixie's mother.

Overhead the gulls called to one another with pitiful cries. The sea, which was the colour of gunmetal, shimmered with a reflected chill as the hours and Ida's slipped beyond life's mystery and pathos. Inside her mansion-block bedroom in Palmeira Crescent the faded upholstery, which had come from Harrods originally, and the foliage and eau-de-Nil walls took on a sober inhabitance. My eye was caught by an assortment of bric-à-brac, family portraits, including one of Roland as an angelic-looking four-year-old, a china-dog eggtimer, boxes of beads, a silver-fox stole and hat-veil, gilt-edged mirrors and plumage. A room, I decided, which revealed little of the true personality of this tiny and frail lady. It was almost a betrayal of her former life and legend on the London stage. Why do people grow old, get ill, wither away and die? Roland says it is how we see ourselves and that we need to correct the illusion. Is cancer an illusion, I ask myself?

I left Roland in Palmeira Crescent while I walked along the sea's edge. I needed the air, needed to watch the white waves jumping over the pebbles, strips of seaweed and torn deckchairs; to note the sea's rage and the wind's fight with it.

'Death must be like this,' I thought, 'and as equally suffocating and enveloping. Is this death I am seeing? Death with its lack of contours.'

There was a sense of detachment from it all. The piers, the pebbles, the playground for summer's children; where were those distractions of amusement now? The sunshades, sticks of rock, Punch and Judy? Where are they now, in the face of memory? Too weary for scrutiny, like the chalked graffiti along the sea wall. When we got back I made us both a cup of tea and placed two slices of bread under the grill for toast. Roland sat quietly, scribbling. I could see him outlining a tree on blotting paper, filling in the contours with lines.

'Emotion lies somewhere between looking and feeling,' he said, marking the roots with a full stop. I didn't answer him. Emotion is emotion and no amount of analysis will make the sadness go away.

We seem preoccupied with time. At least I am. We are still young but are aware of its passing. Especially when the hours go by and the panic sets in. It is a sobering thought that we are little other than dirt, dust and ashes, fated to mutation, age and decay. How transparent people are when we really look at them. Even the coffee stall at Sloane Square was deserted as we turned the corner on the bus. Who was going to eat all those Spam rolls, I wondered?

A tramp rolling a cigarette was loitering with avid concentration in the builders' merchants' doorway opposite. His whole world seemed reduced to the reassembling of the frayed tobacco. Beside him was a cracked mug of tea. A world containing little other than roll-ups and teacups. Yet in that limited perimeter he was probably happier than most.

October 29th A century ago, perhaps less than that, it would not have been safe for a woman to walk alone around these streets. Although the streets are enclosures for some of the solitary, the down-and-outs, with that vacant and protected expression in their eyes, the singular detachment which clouds their view, I feel no anxiety walking among them. Perhaps they sense the concern in my nod of greeting. For some the crowd is all they have, the casual acknowledgement of their presence.

We had to rescue Trixie from the bomb site this evening. She was playing with broken tins, stones, dry mud, old saucepans and wood, and had fallen and hurt herself. Poor mite. I left her playing quietly with Sally, a game they call 'Mothers and Fathers', with an assortment of toys. I finished the ironing and let down the hem of a dress. There is no let-up for the women around here. They are working from the moment they get up in the morning until they go to bed. If they are not cooking, mending, scrubbing, washing, ironing, shopping and looking after their kids, they are ever attending to their husbands' lust.

The whole tenement knows when Gladys and Bob Startup are visiting the public baths down Old Pye Street to wash the curtains because they put newspapers up meantime.

Toby Wentworth called again yesterday evening just as I had finished washing my hair. With head in a towel, I made him a cup of this new instant coffee. Maxwell House, 'America's Favourite Coffee', or so the adverts would have us believe. It comes in the form of brown powder in a little round tin. It is not bad, easy to make and very different from either Camp or Bev, which come pre-sweetened.

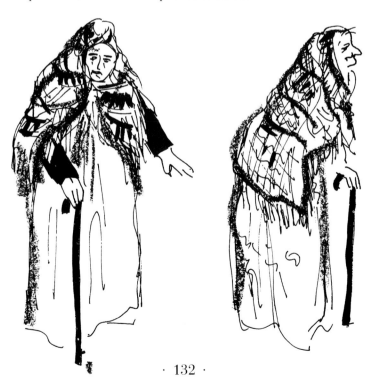

He had been to Paris for a week to visit a sick friend. At least that is what he would have us believe. He said he took the Golden Arrow and ferry over the Channel and was in the heart of Paris by 6 p.m. Paris, the city of Baudelaire, Utrillo and Apollinaire, conjures up images of brightly lit cafés, tree-lined boulevards, intimate bistros, warm bread and cognac, with lovers dining *à deux*.

'My hotel was on the rue du Montparnasse, around the corner from the Café du Dôme,' he told me. Neither I nor Roland has seen Paris, a city he says every writer and artist should visit at least once in their lives.

'It wasn't particularly comfy, but it was clean and warm with plenty of hot water. I never felt so clean, with my own bidet and a window overlooking a mediaeval courtyard.'

Toby, whose excellent graphic recall held me enthralled for several hours, in between a plate of minced meat and cabbage, seemed happier and more relaxed than previously. He enjoyed numerous carafes of rosé, fresh cabbage, browned potatoes, veal and soft cheese. Paris did not appear to be so short of food as London. He described taxi rides down wide, bright boulevards such as the Beaumarchais, Magenta, Rochechouart, into a rouged web of clip-joints, clubs and dives around Place Pigalle. Where pimps hung around corners surveying the scene: a living embodiment to the memory of Toulouse-Lautrec, I thought.

He bought Roland a box containing fifty Disque Bleu cigarettes and myself a vial of Parfum Gemey from a shop along the rue de la Paix. We put him up for the night by tying the two easy chairs together alongside the fire's dying embers. I need not have worried about the problem of getting washed and dressed this morning with our obvious lack of privacy, because when I got up Toby had already gone. The Third Programme played a Concerto for Oboe and Strings by Bach as I sipped my first cup of tea. I had to admit to a feeling of disappointment at Toby's premature departure, but he has always been something of a mystery, a dark horse as they say, and although Roland has known him for years, he has to admit that he doesn't really know him.

'There was a rumour on set that he was attached to MI5, working clandestinely for the West.'

One can never be surprised at anything these days and Toby, who was up at Cambridge before the war, mixed with some strange people. There is something about the unexpected arrival of an attractive man which makes one suddenly conscious of self and of one's immediate surroundings. My hair needs cutting, nails manicuring and my face would not come amiss with a little attention, either.

The priest called tonight, finishing the final slice of my home-made fruit cake. Munching away with animated movements, he was not unlike the puppet-master in *Petrushka* with his sorcerer's cassock and ecclesiastical smile.

*Mr Streetsinger, treading the streets on Sunday afternoons for
a fistful of phlegm and farthings.*

Opposite   *Going home from work past St Matthew's Church, Great Peter Street.*

November 20th I was filled with a morbid sadness today on hearing that Willoughby Cleaver, the poor old shell-shock victim, had been found dead. He had been there for about a week before Rose Sweeny and her husband found him. She was delivering him one of her little food packets and a toffee-apple. He was never without that black attaché case, stomping along and waving his fists. And now he is dead. Roland feels sure he too would end up that way, alone and neglected, destined for the pauper's grave, were it not for me looking after him. Men alone don't seem to survive so well as women. Perhaps it is because they are more used to having mothers, sisters and grandmothers to do things for them.

I will never forget that old man with his sad, troubled eyes which held a universe in their expression. Nor forget his more lucid moments of conversation in a cultured accent which belied a background different from the one he ended up in. Some said he had worked for the BBC World Service as a diplomatic correspondent, and others that he had befriended Vanessa Bell and her Charleston coterie. Somewhere between them is the truth. We are all mirrors and masks living by selected emotions.

Roland gave him his old blue-and-black-checked greatcoat last winter, because it was a little less threadbare than the buttonless, torn one he was wearing. The old chap was so grateful, promptly returning the gesture with a pile of early war editions of Enid Blyton's *Sunny Stories* for Sally. Who would have thought he would have preserved things like that? Sally cried when we told her he had died. I am not sure what the term death means to her, except she sees it as people closing their eyes forever and knows that she may never see them again except in Heaven. Both she and Trixie took him down a packet of bread and dripping one day, which she insisted I make up. They simply knocked at his door and presented it to him. I was worried lest we offend him. In such sensitive situations one has to be careful not to upset another's dignity and pride. Bread and dripping was all we could offer, for our own lunch that day had been reduced to a cup of Edward's desiccated soup with a slice of bread. Roland had had a penny Oxo cube dissolved in a cup of hot water and Sally a packet of Smith's crisps with a blue bag of salt.

During lean times such as this, Roland effectively tightens his belt, figuratively speaking, and looks through his canvases. He endeavours to keep by a few silver-foil-wrapped squares of Bournville chocolate in the pocket of one of his jackets hanging beneath a sheet of brown paper on the bedroom door. He still persists in keeping his entire wardrobe there, mostly cast-offs from the film studios.

'I get nowhere with my art,' he complains in his notes. 'I can never achieve the feeling or emotion which lies behind the appearance of things. Nor can I find adequate solutions to display this eternal rhythm.'

I left him demolishing a packet of five Senior Service cigarettes while I opened a tin of Crosse and Blackwell's baked beans for tea.

November 21st There was a puddle on the floor when I got back yesterday. The kettle had sprung a leak. Hopefully the ironmonger will have one of those metal discs that cover the hole with a nut. 'Make Do and Mend', the magazine articles advise. Our war with its difficulties still continues.

The manageress at the dress shop I work in in Warwick Way gave me some out-of-date fashion catalogues for Sally to amuse herself with. Predictably she went wild with excitement, so great is her enthusiasm for anything designed or colourful, and which allows space for her to copy. All those 1949 full-skirted models with their nipped-in waists and soft, rounded lines inspired by Dior's New Look makes my wardrobe look ancient. Although clothing is now coupon-free, most people in the streets are still having to make do with the skimpy, austere, severe-looking outfits of war and of the immediate post-war period. There isn't the money around, but people appear happy.

During the war I kept a diary of sorts, but not as detailed as this one, and I came across it looking for something else. Whereas Roland keeps his thoughts in suitcases I keep mine in cardboard boxes which occasionally get disturbed, repacked and stored again. Even if I lived in a house the size of Buckingham Palace I would still retain my boxes. I made a small pot of tea for myself and leafed through the pages about our home being bombed in 1941.

I shuddered at the thought and memory of it all. What we lived through, the daily terror, the lack of food, facilities, the ability to get a good wash. I have always believed in fate and instinct. I had had such a strange urge to get home that night. I can't imagine now the shock I would have had to have discovered our house and family gone. We had to leave our possessions and move in elsewhere. Then it was camp beds with thick blankets for months, and endless sandwiches and cups of tea and coffee from large urns. The worst part was the smell. That awful smell of burning, decay and soot. It was everywhere, in my hair, clothes, the bed I slept in. I can smell it even now.

Toby passed through again, having spent the earlier part of the evening in the Plough, Museum Street. He has met a girl, French, called Violette.

November 26th A bout of indigestion kept me awake last night, so I sipped a glass of warm water mixed with a teaspoon of bicarbonate of soda before my tea this morning. It must have been those kippers we had for lunch. I was washing the dishes when I heard the results of a bitter feud going on. Not a nod has passed between Old Irish and Bella Ricketts in months. It seems the two fell out over Old Irish's non-payment of her paper bill, triggering off a multitude of deep-seated grievances. It is hardly surprising that these outbreaks occur from time to time; it's the proximity of us all. Links have been built up since school, street-life and work days; wherever one looks there is someone one knows moving outside, people standing talking on the landings and stairwells, at entrances and street-corners, with this strong day-to-day reliance on their families for companionship rather than seeking it from beyond the tenement's framework. A person alone here, without the extended family network to fall back on, has a harder time. In spite of the sheer volume of human traffic residing here, this camaraderie doesn't extend into the boundary of the individual home. As a rule neighbours are not invited into the home. I suppose this is the only way most are able to maintain a measure of privacy.

With items of new furniture becoming more readily available, those who can afford to are gradually discarding the Utility range in favour of the new Contemporary Look. Payments are by hire purchase. There have been no such changes with us, although I have seen a sideboard in the Army and Navy Stores priced £17 12s 6d. We would get a rebate of 2/- per pound with Roland working there.* It would take about two years to pay off and means the chest of drawers could go into the bedroom where it belongs.

Freddie came to see us on Sunday morning; he cycles over from Ebury Mews whenever he is on weekend leave from National Service. He has had to forgo his accountancy studies for the time being. He arrived with a soap model of Donald Duck for Sally and five Weights for me. Sally wanted the soap to stand on the mantelshelf between the cocoa tin and Roland's red glass of the Sacred Heart. Coloured blue, red and gold, he looks too good to use. Freddie gave her and Trixie turns on the crossbar of his bicycle, peddling past the men on the pavements with their grey faces and even greyer mackintoshes, beside the graffiti, brickwork and advertisements. Beneath the columns of hissing white incandescence which provide Freddie, myself, Sally and Trixie with a simplified view of reality. Tramps in ragged overcoats, old ladies carrying potatoes home in string bags, as the tenement falls away at the edges. A view which almost, but not quite, competes with a living print of Gustave Doré's.

Even Roland recognises that. 'There could be something in this,' he said unexpectedly one evening. 'Maybe I should start placing figures in my landscape.'

I have a few woollens to rinse out with Sylvan Flakes, available in the shops once again, and Sally wants to wash her doll's clothes. The District Nurse visited Frederick Scullion earlier. Perhaps I will give him a knock later and see if there is anything I can do.

*Roland did get a part-time job in the Army and Navy Stores, as Albert Mavrolean suggested.

'Hot pie, tea, two sugars, please mate,' orders Charlie Farmer, shaking the bottle of brown sauce. 'Bit quiet for a Friday night?' Where are the wages this week?

December 1st It is cold today, with a bright sun. There is a portion of stew on the gas stove and half a loaf of bread on the table. Inside the wooden wall-cupboard there are a few rock cakes and a tin of South African peaches. Beside the cutlery box is an opened tin of condensed milk and a packet of custard powder. This is all we have until the next rations are due, apart from a little tea and sugar. Sally helped me line the shelves with flower-patterned wax paper which I bought from the King's Road Woolworth's. While we were doing it we discovered a tray of packets, boxes, folded bags, flavourings and powders going mouldy; so damp is the cupboard that I have to leave it ajar. Neither Sally nor Roland is keen on vanilla blancmange so I will give that away. Both are inclined to be fussy eaters and complain about the skin which forms on warm milk, custard and rice pudding in the cooling process. Then Sally won't touch cheese or bread if it has holes in it. So with a fear of feathers, birds flying around her and the dark, I wonder how she manages to cope at all.

It is a survival course, this life of ours, but no matter how careful we are with what we eat it doesn't prevent us getting ill. Roland had yellow jaundice this year, so badly that he had to go into St Mary Abbott's Hospital in Kensington.

I see Teresa O'Gorman is walking-out with Terry Cox from the Little Square. How quickly children grow up now. One minute they are running around the yard and the next smartening themselves in preparation for courtship. Terry, with his Brylcreamed hair, straightening his tie, and Teresa, in her black louis-heeled pumps, costume and rouged face, journey no further than the twin-seated, horse-hair sofa of his potential in-laws.

While I thus mused, Roland sat in silence, having eaten his boiled potatoes, cabbage and chop. Sometimes his silence is almost secretive. He will be getting out his tin of Cherry Blossom shoe polish next, the two brushes, rag and duster to layer a hint of camouflage on to those scuffed and holed shoes. Much to the amusement of the neighbours, he is wearing his pre-war correspondent shoes these days, the ones he was wearing when I first met him, because they are the only pair he owns which don't let the water in.

December 3rd We have been given our biannual bucket of ready-mixed khaki distemper to redecorate the living room. What a business! It has to be done because Head Office's Annual Inspection is due and there have been no attempts at decorating since we moved in. Distemper is particularly awful because when damp it smells like sour eggs and quickly discolours. The khaki will have turned brown in a year or so. Freddie said he would help when he is next home on leave, so margin by margin, brushline upon focusable brushline, it will cover the peeling surface.

We all complain of fatigue, chronic, unremitting fatigue which hovers like a dark beast over our existence. Any energy we do have remains closeted in preference to exploring new methods, situations and territories. How many of us ascend to the upper deck of buses and go to Oxford Street? That street with its substantial shops, barrows and street-musicians. Or who can quote a line from a book of Andrew Marvell's poems, or pause to look at the sky between the chimney smoke billowing over the rooftops? Not many, if any at all. Mostly our energy remains sapped by a disabling tiredness that even a full night's sleep can't dispel.

One of Roland's quirks is to be prepared for the unexpected, a suitcase packed with a change of clothes. His very own attaché case with seven ties, a notebook plus a tin of Gibb's Dentifrice toothpaste, in case he should find himself summoned in the night to go on location. When I suggested this might be unlikely, as he is not yet a star, especially with the current financial difficulties in the British Film Industry, he responded with sadness: 'Even if one never knows what kind of day tomorrow will be or what mood one will be in, it is important to have the appropriate tie. It is a matter of breeding. Diplomacy.'

Talking of ascension, Iris Meadow's sister Betty got married on Saturday. They held the reception for some two hundred up in the washhouse. I could think of more imaginative places to hold it, but they could make as much noise as they wanted on the concrete floors. One by one the guests trooped up five flights of stairs, dressed in their best attire. Elsie Sumption, Mr and Mrs Sugden and a few of the others went and had the time of their lives performing 'okey-cokeys and knees-ups in and out of the copper boilers and beneath lines of old socks, underpants and pairs of combinations. They were still at it long after the happy couple had left for a honeymoon on Clacton sands.

Mr Lamplighter-Biker has presented Mabel Wagstaffe with a ginger tomcat. I could see her sitting with it curled over her feet. It is strange how no one draws their curtains around here. Walking around the block for a little evening air I can see kids playing, neighbours watching from windows and the balustrades, while others sit on kitchen chairs in attitudes of talking and watching.

> *A walk through this*
> *Dawn Westminster*
> *Combines with shapes*
> *Of cloud and melancholy*

December 12th I stopped to listen to Emily Riggs playing her barrel-organ on Saturday morning, with a repertoire of tunes from my childhood. Emily Riggs. Some say she is twice as old as the century, and judging from her appearance she could well be. I expect she is steeped in the district's history. I think one should talk to characters like this and record their personal stories, because once they die all that information will go with them.

The thought struck me this evening that Roland invariably paints trees and landscapes, but never people. He will spend hours attempting to capture the drab jigsaw of slop-slithering streets with their heavy cloud, appearance of secrecy, ordinariness and enclosure, but never people. So I asked him why.

'They invade my privacy,' he replied. 'Everywhere I look there are people. People crowding out the shops, buses, lighted foyers, walking beneath the neon. It's nothing but a sombre press of people. I need the space.'

Roland is as much a loner on canvas as he is in life. While he contemplates his notes I wonder at those three thousand or so nineteenth-century souls depicted in the Rookery etchings of Gustave Doré with their hint of yesterday's lived-in ugliness, and who seem to gather round him mockingly. Whose expressions seem to suggest that they still live here, inhabiting the very pores of our skin. Vincent Van Gogh wrote in a letter to his brother Theo that a lot of painters go mad. Painting with its quest for truth, search for validity behind the appearance can sometimes leave them vague and absent-minded.

Roland and I took the No. 11 bus to Chelsea Town Hall for the Chelsea Palace of Varieties. A friend of mine works in the ticket office and was able to give us complimentary tickets. I painted my nails with Cutex Cameo nail varnish, and used Angel Face powder on my face. With my black velvet bolero over a red woollen dress with a ruched waist and tulip sleeves, Roland declared I could still give Vivien Leigh and Loretta Young a run for their money. I also wore a string of Roland's mother Katrina's jet and crystal beads.

Jean Farmer once said that many of the neighbours spent most of their Sundays in bed for reasons of boredom, warmth and tiredness. I can't say I blame them. It saves on food and fuel bills, and even Roland has the occasional lie-in some Sundays with the black-out up. Sunday is a strange day to fill during the winter months of cold and darkness. There is very little for people to do except walk around the streets. But they get filled. Some Sundays when at a loose end we go to a Movietone News and Cartoon cosiness of the News Theatre. There are several around but we prefer the one in Victoria Station or the one in Piccadilly. Roland has a 3d tub of vanilla ice-cream while I enjoy the remainder of the week's sweet rations.

I popped over to Mrs Skinner in D Block after tea tonight with a skirt I had altered for her. She has to make do with only one room. The bed, which was unmade, provides a seat at the small square table covered in a grubby cloth. On it was a loaf of uncut bread, what looked like the remains of two days' dirty crockery, a packet of buttons, milk bottles, jug and a cruet set rusting around the top. We faced one another under three lines of drying washing looking the worse for a smoking grate. Mrs Skinner, her hair coiled under a black net, was seated in her dressing gown nervously rolling a cigarette. She offered me one, apologising for the state of the room.

'It's difficult to keep it clean when there's no place to put anything,' she said. I understood that perfectly. She suggested a cup of tea but when I saw the colour of the dish-cloth used to wipe the cups, I declined. I left later with a feeling that Mrs Skinner spent most of her days slopping around between bed, table and hearth and back again. Her room, with its appearance of sadness and neglect, seemed to inhale the collective sour odours of our narrow existence.

December 18th I am still doing the washing, except the sheets, by hand. The women still trundle off, regular as clockwork, to the public baths down the bottom of Old Pye Street. They go like participants in a carnival procession, with their piles of dirty linen stacked in tin baths, which in turn are balanced on ancient prams and pushchairs. It is a wonderful sight. A testament to tenement life, with their jugs of tea, packets of cheese sandwiches, mob-caps, and cigarettes dangling from their mouths.

Claudine has finally selected a date for her wedding, which will be in Fulham Registry Office, Walham Green. Mother wanted her to marry at St Michael's, Chester Square, but Claudine said she preferred not to have all the fuss.

I went with her to choose her wedding-suit pattern and cloth at Willerby's in Victoria Street. She selected an elegant pale-blue worsted and a pair of black suede court shoes from Dolcis next door to the Cameo Cinema and Zeeta's Restaurant. As a treat for Sally and Roland, we bought a Fuller's walnut layer cake, stopping first to enjoy a pot of tea in their cafeteria.

I still spend most of my evenings sewing, mending, unpicking garments or unravelling bits of old wool. Neighbours who hear that I can do things like this bring me their unwanted bags of wool and material patches. Although my Singer treddle sewing machine goes well, I still miss those Wilcox and Gibbs power machines we had in the workrooms at Woolland's. I can still see Mr Norman Woolland in my mind's eye, a portly gentleman standing silently watching us all. He had been something of a big-shot in he RAF, I heard. He would stand looking over us like a casting director searching for signs of talent in the chorus-line.

I can hear the kids shrieking in the street, chasing one another and outdistancing Mr Cornelius Wilby as he enters by the White Arch. 'Got any sweets, Mr Wilby? Got any sweets?' I wish I could boast of holidays in a villa in Menton, south of France. But then a caravan at Bognor wouldn't come amiss either.

DANCING DOWN OLD PYE STREET

1951

A splash of burnt umber
As tissue-wafer leaves
And London walks into
The next hour

January 1st What a bleak time of the year this is with snow, fog, wind and rain threatening over the macadam like a writhing greasy eel. June Flynn the paper-round girl went off as usual at 6.30 a.m. Come rain or sun I don't think that poor kid has ever missed a morning. It can't be easy going out into a frozen dawn to deliver, she tells me, three rounds which include Buckingham Gate, the Artillery Mansions and Westminster Palace Gardens. I can hear Bella Ricketts going off to the barber's shop in Palmer's Alley. I write this down because it is the only item of news today. I took Sally in the pushchair and went to take a peep through the steamed-up window. And sure enough, there she was, sitting between two male patrons in a wooden chair, bibbed and towelled and awaiting the barber's clippers.

January 9th So has Roland anything to protect his dreaming? Very little, it would seem. And he still doesn't possess a wardrobe, making full use of the hook on the back of the bedroom door; laying out his washing and shaving kit each night in strict, barrack-room fashion. There is his collection of Tchaikovsky and *Les Sylphides*, seventy-eight records with no gramophone to play them on. A hint of what existed in his earlier life, the one he knew before his world of gold alchemised into one of bitumen. The Putney Common, Barnes, America and Denham Studio days, locked now into bundles and fragments for a life once lived. And his coughing is getting worse; lungs choked with dust, disappointment and despair.

'Want anything, Mister? Want any Weights, Woodbines, snuff or Turf? We'll get them for you Mister.' One of the many local errand-runners performs the nightly ritual of knocking on the door in hope of earning the luxury of a thruppenny bit, thus contributing to the addiction.

Then Belinda called round in tears. Her affair has ended, as I knew it would. It ran out of steam, or he had, she said.

'There were others. He told me I was different, that I really understood him.' 'Don't they all?' I thought cynically. My little sister, I fancy, had been obsessed by the romance of it, the opportunity, however small, it afforded her to try something different. He left her a month's rent for the Percy Street flat and returned to his wife, just like they always do until the next time. Men can be such emotional cowards. Perhaps that is why so many select marriage with boring, undemanding women, taking occasional excursions into passion, intrigue and excitement in short-lived bursts. There can be little to beat the sheer luxury of intoxication that having someone fall in love with us brings. That is the bonus of infidelity.

I think time will help her, and loving will have made her a more full person. Love unleashes a precious experience of the beautiful by allowing us to focus on the beautiful. It is in the experience of true beauty that we find satisfaction; for loving is an act of entrustment.

January 28th The Festival of Britain is due to open in May with the hope that it will blow away those final, lingering cobwebs and hardships of war. The aim is for a celebration in an enclosure of colour and light. Directed by Gerald Barry and the architect Hugh Casson, a space has been allocated alongside the River Thames between County Hall and Waterloo Bridge. By way of pavilions and displays it will tell the story of Britain, its land and people, and the British role in exploration and discovery.

Roland placed a pair of sheets in the pawn shop on Saturday, a pair I had been saving since our wedding for the day when we moved. It was like an omen. To cheer ourselves up we shared a box of violet-scented cachous and had a glass of tonic wine. For some reason I find myself longing for a chocolate biscuit.

It is raining again. Cold, wet, windy and January. Not the sort of day to go walking around the streets, so I gave myself a face-pack with fuller's earth, manicured my nails and had an early night. Tomorrow, if it is brighter, I will go along the Embankment to watch the Festival building-work in progress. Have a look at the pylon all the newspapers are talking about. The reports say that lack of material and other shortages have meant work is behind schedule. There will be more activity in Battersea. An acre of beautiful trees and shrubberies will be uprooted to make way for the erection of Pleasure Gardens, which, it is hoped, will emulate those eighteenth-century versions of Vauxhall and Ranelagh, and a Funfair. 'A place where', as Gerald Barry expresses it, 'people can relax and have fun, some elegant fun.'

Apart from bread, milk and sandwiches, coffee, cocoa and tea, people go into the Dairy for glasses of lemonade and ginger beer and to watch Maurice ladling out the milk.

February 3rd

> *Stark moon with frozen*
> *Sienna. Fermentation*
> *Crushed breath.*
> *Winter with life continuing,*
> *Just.*

They have emptied Willoughby Cleaver's room, flung out the iron bedstead with its sagging springs. Roland enquired about his attaché case with its notes and copies of the old man's dispatches. But someone had been there before him.

I forgot to write a note for Alec the milkman to leave an extra half a pint, so now there won't be enough for the morning. The doctor suggested I was going through a phase and should not worry about it. These feelings of hopelessness and melancholy which sweep over me from time to time. What does he know? Men don't get these things like we do, don't understand the emotional ordeal of having a miscarriage.

To make a change, Sally and I had lunch in the Playfoot Dairy in the market. It is a pleasant brother-and-sister-run business, with a couple of friendly ladies helping out during their busy periods. They live over the Dairy in Dacre Chambers. The Dairy is kept immaculate and its blue, white and majolica-patterned wall-tiles remind me of the William Morris-designed restaurant in the Victoria and Albert Museum. The milk is ladled out from a large china urn standing on the marble-topped counter. Customers bring their own jugs, as pint and half-pint measures of milk are bought, or placed on tick. The Dairy was the first along the market to stock the new sliced bread by Lyons, wrapped in blue-and-white-check paper. Sally likes going in there because the dairy-man, or Maurice-the-Milk, as Roland calls him, makes a fuss of her by wanting to cut off one of her red curls. He invariably gives her a sticky iced bun, which she proudly runs home with to share with me. Once she dropped it in the mud and howled for hours. In the end I had to go back and buy us one each to pacify her.

Winter has brought a stillness to the tenement, which sits within it like a rusty cage, its inhabitants seeking refuge beneath it. In spite of its grim, barrack-like appearance, the cell-sized rooms, toil of lavatory and water-tap sharing, and cleaning of public areas, the closeness and success of its community lies with its inhabitants. The friendship between them, family to family, and each household of people to one another, is a feat beyond expectation. They get through the monotony of days because they share their troubles, confide in one another, drawing on a collective experience and support.

February 23rd I have been having broken nights again, worrying about the future, Sally, Roland, where it is going to end. The night hours seem endless, tossing and turning, listening to the street drunks calling one another, the down-and-outs arguing; the tenement rows amid the sound of a ravaging wind.

To save coal we are being advised to reduce the size of our fireplaces by placing a brick at the back and one on either side of the grate. I sent Roland out to search for spare bricks on the bomb site at the top end of Great Peter Street and he came back with more than that. Someone had dumped a suitcase of books containing a library more considerable than a Charing Cross Road bookshop, with the works of Chaucer, Blake and Baudelaire among them.

'It pays to be on the look-out for the unexpected,' he remarked with the demeanour of someone seeking to grow, identify himself more fully with life.

March 8th They have a new parish priest over at St Ann's, a Monsignor, and he knocked at the door the other night. He came to sift through the line and tone of his motley neighbourhood Catholic family. A nice man, I thought, with a gentle smile, dark eyes and a shy, unassuming manner. I liked him immediately. Some of them would make such lovely husbands and companions, and he is one of them.

He talked about marriage, declaring how a married couple can make such an important contribution to the unity and continuing stability of society by remaining faithful to their promises of lifelong fidelity. He had that special way with him that both attracts and instantly warms one to him. He would be a good friend and spiritual counsellor for Roland, as he didn't take to the other priest. They have their moments, like the rest of us. Sally established an instant rapport by showing him her drawings and giving him a hug. Her friend Trixie had been showing her how to form the letters of the alphabet. How they must miss having children of their own. Their vocation cannot be an easy one. I found myself hoping he would call again soon, attracted by that easy manner, quiet solicitude, intelligence and calm. The affinity he afforded me with that sudden rush of recognition which is kinder, more lasting than passion.

If I am quick I can rub in a few fruit buns for tea to make a change from that stodgy fruit cake Belinda brought back from Bath. I had asked her to get a lardy cake, but there we are.

April 2nd The mantelshelf remains filled with the usual bric-à-brac, documents, letters, clock, rent receipts, bits of jewellery, photos, our ration books and Roland's observance of the Sacred Heart. Whenever I want to compose a letter, cut out some material, or write this diary, I have to clear a section of the kitchen table. There is never a moment when it is not in use. I scrub its wooden surface at least twice a week and cover it with American cloth. When Sally drapes an old sheet over it, it becomes a make-believe house; she climbs beneath it with her toys and teddy bear. It can take on the reality of a schoolroom, hospital or boat rocking on the high seas, according to which story has currently caught her imagination. Especially those inspired by *Listen with Mother*.

We are sending her to ballet classes at the Mayfair School of Dancing in Wilfred Street. She loves to dance and swirl around in her blue tunic with its circular skirt. Roland would have liked to send her to stage school, for in addition to drawing and painting she is a born mimic. She won a Talent Competition organised by one of those Holidays at Home shows last summer when they visited Old Pye Street.

The latest in games crazes around here is for an activity colloquially referred to as 'Gobs'. It comprises five small cubic stones in different colours. These are skilfully used as a multiplicity of single-handed, juggling acts which are performed in turn. One sees groups and pockets of youthful absorption on the stairs, passages, landings and yard surfaces, each patiently waiting their turn. If they could get on the roof they would be playing up there too.

I found myself thinking once more of Willoughby Cleaver and the sad, lonely end to his life. There are probably many like him, hidden away in secret pockets, lamenting their lost youth and missed opportunities, although I don't think he did, so patient in his afflictions.

A man standing in front of the Railway Lost Property Office in Victoria Street selling balloons caught my eye. Feeling reckless I bought a red one for 3d.

'Good for you, lady,' he said, searching in his pocket for change. 'It's time to be happy, say hello to the traffic and have yourself a glass of wine.' I smiled at him and bought a blue balloon as well. 'Life is a celebration and should be celebrated. Good luck to you, lady.'

Thus spoke this erstwhile pavement philosopher, whose comments inadvertently reminded me that on the South Bank this summer, a celebration it will be.

May 3rd The day has arrived. The Festival of Britain 1951 has been officially opened today and will run until 30th September. It looks extraordinary from this side of the Thames. We went to watch the fireworks, dancing and general air of gaiety. There will be dancing every night for those with stamina after a day's work. A place where people can collide. Not everyone can be rich, happy, successful, lucky or beautiful all the time, but they can pretend to be.

One family around here produces a new child annually. Twins arrived this year, bringing the total so far to eleven. They rent two adjoining rooms, filled, I am told, with an array of home-made bunk-beds.

'We sleep four in there, three in here, four next door and two up the bleeding chimney,' the father was overheard to say. Judging by the colour some of them go to school, no doubt through the lack of washing facility and time in the mornings, that remark might not be an exaggeration.

May 29th The problem of Sally's schooling will arrive next year. Roland wants her to have a private education like himself, something convent-based, but if we can't afford it it will need to be one of the local schools. There is one still referred to by its original name of 'Townshend Ragged'; a school set up by the Board of Education last century to comply with the 1870 Education Act. There is the local church school in Old Pye Street, which is close to the site of the nineteenth-century branch called the One Tun Ragged. What a choice! The Catholic school is a little too rough.

In a light mood I put on my new cotton frock, white sandals and, with Sally in a matching outfit, took the bus to Trafalgar Square. We spent the afternoon wandering around the National Portrait Gallery, feeding the pigeons in Leicester Square, and stopping for a snack in Cranbourn Street, a cream-and-green place with adverts for foreign films and posters displaying bottles of Coca-Cola. I searched the shelves of Zwemmer's Art Bookshop for something suitable for Roland's birthday next month, eventually deciding on a second-hand collection of lithographs by Toulouse-Lautrec from a curio shop in Cecil Court. Sitting beside the fountains in Leicester Square, listening to a busking jazz, be-bop group, I thought to myself: 'This is life. This is life this moment, May 29th 1951.'

The men in their crêpe-soled shoes, gabardines, check shirts, loud ties, and the women wearing modified versions of cocktail dresses, pump shoes; some are lying asleep or watchful, hand-touching along with other aspects of the *mise-en-scène* that lovers use to declare love. When the wind started up we made for home, crossing by Admiralty Arch and cutting through St James's Park. We met Gladys and Bob Startup near the suspension bridge, feeding the herons. 'Hello, ducks,' they greeted me somewhat appropriately. 'Nice day then, eh?'

Indeed it was I thought. A nice day for the ducks.

Palmer's Passage – always known as Palmer's Alley – narrow and dark.

June 5th Sally and I still do the trek to Ebury Mews, mostly in the evenings now to avoid explanations of our plight should we bump into former friends and acquaintances. Jeremy would be appalled, I know. Mother and I sit talking while Sally plays downstairs in the mews. Sometimes there are a few other children to play with her, but mostly she is alone with her skipping rope and crayons. There is only Poppy at home now and she is always out with some new sailor boyfriend or other who happens to be home on leave. We discuss this and that; the neighbours, economy recipes, the situation with Belinda, that kind of thing. And especially what Freddie will do when National Service ends as he hasn't completed his chartered accountancy exams yet.

I bought a copy of *John Bull* and *Everybody's Weekly* magazines and a pair of herrings, then settled down for an evening of reading, knitting and listening to the wireless. What do we live for? From habit, fear, a sense of obligation, I found myself wondering? Next February Princess Elizabeth and Prince Philip will start a tour of the Commonwealth, as the former Empire is now being called. I wonder what their answers would be to those questions, living, as they do, a mere stone's throw away from us. And if I could buy the new £30 Hoover electric washing machine available on HP terms advertised in this magazine, I might have a little more time to think and find answers. But as yet we don't even have the electricity to run a washing machine.

During the long summer months, and mostly on Sunday afternoons, we are plagued with a succession of streetsingers and visiting roundabout men who offer the kids rides in exchange for pennies, rags or old metal. Some provide competitions from which a successful child will come away with a goldfish swimming around in a plastic bag of water. A head-count on the numbers of goldfish swimming around the Artillery Mansions forecourt fountain on Monday mornings would find their numbers greatly increased. Generally Sunday is a day for the dynastic families living in the nearby lodging houses to parade their finery on their way to church. Out they come one by one, like boxes of coloured Allsorts in their bonnets, bows, satins and silk in a seventh-day attempt to look respectable. Whenever they appear I am reminded of the song 'Buttons and Bows'; it seems particularly apt.

July 20th Roland has been to the barber's shop in Palmer's Alley where Bella Ricketts goes for her haircut. He is happy at the moment, having learnt that he has a small part in *Twelve Days to Noon*, which will involve some early-morning location shots around Westminster Bridge. He'll be able to pop home for breakfast.

I seem to spend a lot of my hours walking up and down Victoria Street, which forms part of my escape route, with Sally and pushchair in tow. When it was first opened in 1851 it was described as one of the sights of London; the most continental street in England, if only by contrast to the narrow streets and alleys through which it was driven, opening up magnificent views of the then new Houses of Parliament. Most of this area was a swamp and, like Buckingham Gate, had to be raised seven feet above its former level. Roland likes this street because of the increasing number of gentlemen's outfitters it affords for him to study; the style of the mansion blocks, and buildings such as Windsor House, which was previously a hotel. When he isn't looking in the windows admiring the latest cut in the suits, he is around the back viewing the clerical vestments in the holy shops, which stand opposite the Cathedral.

I bumped into Mr Pashkoff, Mr Cornelius Wilby's friend from the Artillery Mansions, in the Army and Navy Stores Aquarium Department.

'I like to watch the little blighters swimming around,' he told me in reference to the fish. 'Damn pretty assistants too. Very knowledgeable about the keeping of pets,' he declared with a roar of a laugh. Mr Pashkoff, it seems, lives for the night. The daytime is something to be got through, like cough linctus, dozing in the chair for the most part with dreams overlapping his more wakeful thoughts. He looked eager for a little company, so when he invited me to join him for a cup of coffee in the Caxton Coffee House I accepted. He looked drawn and pale, with his ragged beard and black beret worn at an angle. We talked for about an hour, he smoking black Russian cigarettes and me spooning shapes in the sugar bowl. I could see from the window the outline of an old man sitting on the tree-seat near the Bluecoat School. In his cloth cap he reminded me a little of Mr Shell-Shock Victim, Willoughby Cleaver, and I found myself telling Mr Pashkoff about him.

'It's a sad world,' he said at length. 'You know you're alone when no one makes any enquiries about you should you go missing, or', he added, 'you remain dead for over a week before anyone finds you.'

August 31st To amuse Sally and Trixie, Roland has devised and made them a pack of cards called Solitary Families, as opposed to the happy variety played by countless generations, and has based his characters on a few of the neighbours. The cards keep them absorbed and laughing for hours and are brought out to show all guests. There is Mr Lamplighter-Biker, old Mother Stout-Guzzler, old Widow Organ-Grinder, Mrs Streetwatcher, Alice Lonely-Heart and Mrs Toffee-Apple Maker to name a few. He can turn his hand to things like this quite happily, but what he really fears is his continuing empty canvas.

What he could not depict in the humour of his line, colour and contours was the real solitariness, the loneliness behind the façade. Nor the fog, smog, snow, wind and rain which regularly tills this former Devil's Acre, this tightly wrapped, black London parcel.

Walking in the cool of memory
There is a need to be still
To make possible silence and
allow the confetti to fall.
Where it will

Mother gave me a tin of sardines which we had tonight on toast. And later, after a walk around the West End, we stopped for a cup of tea from a stall at the foot of Villiers Street by Charing Cross, where night-workers, prowlers, ladies of the pavement, young men in evening dress also enjoyed sardine-filled sandwiches with the aplomb of habitués. It is a warm night with a summer moon outlining the buildings. Far too beautiful to return to the stuffiness of our rooms. Along the Embankment the pavement artists have been at work with moonlit scenes: the Moulin Rouge, can-can dancers, circus clowns and portraits. Roland thought them magnificent. We hoped they had made at least a few pennies for their efforts.

September 12th It is almost time for the BBC's *Nine O'Clock News* so I had better clear away the breakfast things and get on with the ironing. I see Roland's left the toilet roll on full view on the sideboard again, next to Sally's pink satin ballet shoes. What a combination. He is the first to complain when he gets all the way down to the WC to discover he has forgotten it. He is back at the Army and Navy Stores for the time being, taking tea-break snacks of bread and marmalade with him in the morning, which give him wind, he says. I used the Lyons' cut loaf from the Playfoot Dairy, sending Sally round with Trixie, plus sixpence and three farthings folded into a small square of paper. She knows that the white-and-blue-check wrapper is the cut loaf, and the pink the uncut. Making the bed and tidying the bedroom, I noticed Roland's tin cup, razor, square of green soap and hairbrush left on the wicker table, which isn't like him. He is generally very tidy. And he isn't painting. Where can he paint? We can't have oil painting here because the smell is overpowering. And Denham is closing so there won't be much in terms of future film-work. He also says that his 'juvenile-lead'-type looks are going out of fashion, although he stood in recently for Derek Bond.

The new parish priest called again, staying over two hours. I felt he was someone I had known all my life, and the fact that I am not a Catholic didn't perturb him. There have been times in his life, he told me, when he too has entertained doubts. Doubts about his faith, his calling, whether he has got it all wrong. Even the most holy of priests have their moments, even when offering up the Body and Blood at the High Altar. It can be a test of their fidelity and faith. As he talked I watched him, noting his troubled, tired eyes, the slenderness of his body, which suggested activity, the need to keep busy with anything and everything that would prevent time with himself. He alone, I thought, would understand why Roland had had to say no to his call.

When he had gone I remembered the shabbiness of the room, the toilet roll on the sideboard, evidence of our dinner on the gas stove, and felt foolish. This is not how we are, and I wanted to call after him. But he had gone, cloaked and hatted into the gathering dusk.

'It is in love', he said, 'that we come to know God, and in beauty His presence.'

September 28th I often think it would make a change to eat out sometimes, try one of those small, clean-looking restaurants along Victoria Street, or one near the Caxton Coffee House in Brewer's Green. There used to be a café in Knightsbridge near the

Victoria Street is full of little teashops and cafés.

British Restaurant which did a tasty Vienna steak; I enjoyed meals there with some of the girls from Woolland's. However, we did manage a visit to a Lyons' Corner House in Coventry Street for three Knickerbocker Glories on Sally's birthday. They were served on a silver tray by a multi-buttoned Nippy. Sally commented to her on the number of buttons, glad none of her dresses had that many to do up.

'They're all right, dearie,' the Nippy said. 'You get used to then, apart from when you're in a hurry.'

I try to have a little fish on Fridays, mainly because of Roland's religion and because Sally likes the red-faced, jovial fishmonger called Fred, who lets her wear his straw-boater hat when we go in. Fred-the-Fish, as Roland somewhat irreverently calls him. He prefers smoked haddock, Sally a kipper, while I resort to a simple white plaice such as old Mother Stout-Guzzler, Agnes Tillett, gives her cat, also called Fred.

Seasonal notes

Eau-de-Nil
Saffron
Sage
Cerise and magenta
On withering leaves

September 29th We enjoyed a feast of Brussels sprouts and roast chestnuts this evening, courtesy of one of the market-traders who had left a pile on his barrow for whoever wanted them.

The nights are beginning to draw in once again, and the thought of winter's arrival fills me with dread. These places are not impossible to keep warm on account of their smallness, but it is the damp, that enervating, deep-seated dampness, which is the worst.

An article I read in the doctor's waiting room stated that the condition of melancholy is some fatal inheritance, whose weakness increases from generation to generation. Elsie Sumption noticed my wan face and commented on it. 'Maybe you should try for another baby,' she suggested, wearing a snuff-coloured suit. 'My old mother always believed there's nothing like giving life to restore one's own faith in life.' She is right, of course. Giving birth and being responsible for a new life changes one for ever. Elsie is one of the local characters, one of the Grafton pub's habitués who consumes pints of Guinness while completing the *Evening News* crossword. She sits there night after night, sniffing and sighing in front of the contents of her bag, her worldly goods, comprising a pair of spectacles, purse, string bag and Bible, assembled on the table.

'When I get browned off, I get out my papier mâché. I learnt it at school,' she said. 'Wallow in it, I do. All that paper, paste, water and greasing dishes with Vaseline. I know what it's like, love,' fixing me with a studious look. 'The days when the afternoon is merely an interlude between lunch and tea.'

I have discovered a place where I can sit and be quiet. The Army and Navy Stores has a reading-cum-rest room. A faded version of a drawing room in a gentlemen's club, such as those one finds around Pall Mall.

September 30th There are times these days when the claustrophobia of it all becomes so intense I could scream, moments when I could cheerfully open up the brickwork and climb through the mortar. There is nowhere to put anything and nowhere for us to go. We sit on top of one another and it is small wonder tempers get frayed.

It can be said that what we are looking for in a sense determines what we see. So with that in mind, this morning I am resolved to smile over our woes and clear the view for some of the looking. I actually did feel happier as the day progressed. Ella Bonsor started talking when I met her at the sink. She has had her problems. Her husband Ernie is from the north of England and they travel everywhere by motor cycle. She sits in the tiny side-car. Like Jean and Charlie Farmer before them, they too work on the London Underground. He runs the ticket office at the Elephant and Castle, while she collects tickets by the turnstiles at Bank station. Mrs Bonsor is always there to help a person in need, but mostly they keep to themselves. She has a soft spot for Sally and often pops a new thruppenny-bit or a shiny sixpence into her hand. 'Buy Teddy a present,' she says.

She made me laugh with a description of how Ernie consumed his whole week's ration of eggs, butter, bacon and marmalade in one sitting. 'He wanted to eat the way he used to,' she said. 'Like he did before the war. The old guts spent the rest of the week in bed with the belly-ache.'

> *To the right sleep*
> *To the left, life*
> *In this block sitting*
> *Lying within ourselves*

October 7th The Festival of Britain ended today with over eight million people having gone to celebrate Britain's future. It seems only yesterday I wrote that it had opened. All that planning and now it is over. Sally loved the Battersea Funfair which Freddie, Poppy and Patricia took her too. They likened it to a large, sophisticated circus with its Tree Walk, Oyster Creek Railway and carriages named Nellie, Neptune and Wild Goose.

The colours of the autumn leaves are magnificent, linking the trees together like lines of festival bunting. A confetti view to alleviate some of the gloom in my head.

Life is a day-to-day affair and every family has its own version of old Mr Tyler's china swan of pennies. Those coins put away for that proverbial rainy day, or periods of illness, to help eke out the new National Health sickness payments. It is how we get by. How we manage with loose change, tick and the tally-man, while remaining impassive to the sundry delights of fried Spam, dried egg and a cup of Oxo dissolved in hot water. The Liza Kinsmans of this world, who, flexing their arm muscles by taking in washing to earn a few bob, remind me of Dostoevsky's heroines.

I went to a jumble sale at St Matthew's Church and salvaged a 1904 edition of *The Life of St Teresa*, which delighted Roland.

A soft fall movement
Lingers within the sky's
Unblemished calm.
Autumn

October 15th There is a family living in one of the lodging houses nearby who hold noisy parties, or rather raucous brawls, every Saturday night. Crateload upon crateload of ale goes in, and then someone starts playing a tune on the honky-tonk piano. From around eleven, when the pubs turn out, others join in the singing, stamping their feet and shouting through a repertoire of old London tunes. The pattern is always the same, expressed with aggression and interspersed with trips into the street to throw up in the gutter. This continues until around 4 a.m., when the police in a Black Maria arrive to take them away. Several of those in attendance live in this block, so if we should complain or start a petition to have the parties banned, we would probably get our door kicked in. They are best described as a rough lot, emerging from generations of costers, stevedores and dockworkers.

I still find myself wondering over the mystery flat and who once lived there. One day I will ask Mr Horace the porter and see what he says. Knowing his sarcasm, he will probably declare it to have been a Fifth Columnist, or Russian spy, who, given a discreet tip-off, slipped out of the country one night, bound for foreign parts by way of the shipping offices in Cockspur Street.

I have been knitting mother a bed-jacket to fill time during these long evenings when there is not much on the wireless. Sally is asleep and Roland is out. I have just seen Ruby O'Keefe go out, resplendent in black taffeta, which crinkled as she walked. I peeped from behind the bedroom curtain as she disappeared around the corner of Old Pye Street. I returned to the living room and emptied the contents of my handbag, separating the items into groups. With a little determination I too could put on a good face! Locating the box of matches on top of the cereal packet, I lit the gas to make a weak pot of tea, and washed my face.

It seems that Belinda is back with her married man, in spite of our warnings. I worry for her because happiness cannot be built on unhappiness, and if this man really loves her he would let her go. He has to make decisions about the future of his marriage without involving her, or having her named in a civil action. The new priest expressed it so well in a recent homily, I thought:

'Being loved is God's finger on your shoulder. There is no peace equivalent to the peace of loving and being loved.' By those free, really free to love us, I could have added. I daresay this man is unhappy with his marriage and by burying himself in work he is avoiding making a decision. But he will have to do something rather than continue in this uncertainty, which is making Belinda unhappy.

October 20th The Conservative Party has won the General Election with Sir Winston Churchill back as Prime Minister. I wonder if any of Roland's relatives in America will send us another of those wonderful food parcels like they did after the war. They have tremendous admiration for Sir Winston and will be happy he is back in office. I remember the day poor old Mr Shell-Shock Victim, Willoughby Cleaver, went to collect his food parcel from the Welfare Clinic at Ebury Bridge. He was so excited, like a little boy, as he waited to catch the No. 11 bus. He came to show us his box of goodies when he returned. We were just as excited for him, the poor soul.

There was a deal of consternation over in the rent office this week when a notice declaring the annual Head Office Inspection went up. This inspection serves two functions. Firstly, to check the tenant actually lives on the premises and is not sub-letting; secondly, that the premises are not being used for business purposes. There is also a third and unspoken reason, which is to inspect for cleanliness. The last time we had an inspection, several of the rooms upstairs had to be sealed off and fumigated. Never do those buckets, mops, brooms and dusters come so quickly into use, with vast quantities of disinfectant swirling around in galvanised pails. George the Greengrocer, who knows a few of the people here, said he had never seen such a collection of old junk as existed in some of their homes. 'Ought to be burnt. Got the worm in it,' he said. 'It's so old, I reckon it came with the Boer War, like most of them did,' he joked.

I shuddered, visualising our Utility furniture. Those who moved in when we did, and for whom the tenement was a first home, chose items from a catalogue. Those who moved in at the turn of the century and during the 1880s are probably still making do. Few have known the real comfort of linoleum or rugs. One or two have these home-made rag rugs, but little else. I have been on the look-out for bits of lino myself to fill sections of uncovered floor, carrying it in after dark. The effect is like a rejected design for a crazy-paving pathway. Rather that than have Sally get splinters in her feet.

October 27th Roland has had a letter at last from Toby, postmarked Paris. He is staying with Violette.

'London's much dirtier than Paris,' it read. 'Violette has introduced me to the poetry of Paul Verlaine, is transforming pots of meat, potatoes, and onions into the most splendid cuisine in her attic flat overlooking the Boulevard Raspail.' While reading this we were dining on a meal of bread and cheese, with the remains of Wednesday's rabbit stew.

Everyone seems to be out of London. Claudine and her husband, who are staying in their caravan at Bognor, have invited us for the weekend. A handful of blue-and-orange days have left me longing for a change of view. My brother Freddie had to lend me the charabanc fare as Roland was down to his last shilling. It made me sad, because it would have been a much-needed break for him as well.

The Embankment coffee stall at the foot of Villiers Street, around the corner from the Savoy.

October 31st We have been going through a rough period, with me feeling mortified at having to ask Freddie for a loan. Nevertheless, Sally and I went to Bognor with a change of clothing, a jigsaw puzzle, a book of fairy stories and my knitting. I left Roland with a box of Shredded Wheat, a tin of baked beans and three days to get up to his own devices. This was Sally's first trip out of London, her first coach ride and visit to the seaside. Needless to say, she was a fidget on the long and bumpy journey, observing that she had never seen so many trees before. Both sides of the road were full of them for most of the journey. The caravan, although small, is neat and compact, affording a measure of privacy and has a central partition.

The night air was so still with its silence, I remained awake for hours. My eyes followed the violet clouds sweeping through a full hunter's moon. The change in the air left me drowsy. One forgets how dirty London air is until one leaves it. I spent most of the weekend lazing in a deckchair while Sally amused herself with a bucket and spade. Claudine and her husband are still in that exhilarated phase where they have eyes only for each other. There was a panic for a while when Sally buried Mr Putney, her teddy bear, in the sand and couldn't find him when the time came to dig him up again. We returned to London on Monday with a bag of potatoes and mushrooms freshly picked from the field where the caravan is parked. The farmer gave us some cabbages from a field where they were about to be ploughed back.

Bognor is a long stretch of a place, with grey twists of streets, stone cottages with curtains drawn against the wind. I found myself in a little church tucked in a side-street. For some reason I had expected it to be shut. I pushed open the door and went inside. It was empty. A secret place waiting for me. As I slipped into a pew near the back, something the Monsignor at St Ann's said echoed through its peaceful enclosure.

'Be still and grow silent. Let God speak within you.'

And in that little church I believe He did. I lit three candles: one for Sally, one for Roland and one for the Monsignor. I offered a prayer for those living in small pockets of isolation in the tenement. For those whose lives had sought a measure of completeness but had not achieved it; and for those who lived in mystery. I also thanked Him for those little things, those unexpected gifts which come free. A sunny day, the sudden smile from a stranger, shared laughter and love amid the undulating shadows of hedgerow, pavement ragwort, daisy and brick.

Mother met us at Victoria and we went for a cup of tea in an Italian café in Elizabeth Street. It had been raining, leaving the puddles full. Sally had a small plate of chips which she expertly brought back up again on the pavement outside. The coach journey had been bumpy. Mother and I had a toasted corned-beef sandwich. I am feeling more refreshed by our small vacation than I have done in months. For the time being, the fluff can remain unswept beneath the beds along with my mending, such as Roland's frayed collar and cuffs; and the weekly wash and washing-up he is sure to have left.

Dancing Down Old Pye Street, 1951

Wet ground and puddles
People pressed together
In rooms.
London is sinking fast.

November 1st Another month and another week beginning. It rained all day, washing the gutters and yard free of dust and rubbish, together with those street-aimed ablutions which cascade down some nights from a tenant's slop-pail on the fourth floor. A tenant too lazy to walk down the passage to the loo. And I don't have an umbrella since I left mine on the No. 11 bus to World's End.

Roland is engaged upon research in the British Museum Reading Room and I am running up a trousseau for a friend of Belinda's. We linked this evening for a walk along the Embankment by New Scotland Yard.

There have been more tourists in London this year and many seem determined to stay. We have Italians, Hungarians, Greek and Turkish Cypriots, with refugees from the Middle and East European zones and the Caribbean, bringing individual and cosmopolitan influences with them as inch by inch, elbow to elbow they snip at the threads of our insular inhabitance with expressions which seem to suggest: 'This is how I look, this is what I am and this is what I can do.'

Teresa Mavrolean, a fifteen-year-old niece of our neighbour Albert's, has got herself a job as a junior clerk at Ambrose Wilson, the corset-maker in Vauxhall Bridge Road. Albert was as pleased as punch. 'She's starting with a five-day week, a bonus and holiday with pay,' he said, 'and they provide a good canteen. Not like in my day.' Teresa has stunning looks and is both tall and willowy with the sloe-eyed, sultry demeanour of a youthful Cleopatra. The girls from this background have only a brief period of flowering when they can dress up, go on dates, dance or visit the cinema free from those responsibilities that time and marriage will eventually impose on them. That is before their youthful prettiness transforms, under a miscellany of tenement chores, into lines of premature ageing.

Bedtime reading tonight is Doris Leslie's *Polonaise*, a novel about the strange love-affair between George Sand and Frederick Chopin. Closing the window, I glanced up the street, observing Violet Clixby, Mrs Streetwatcher's silent silhouette leaning out from hers. How alone that woman seems.

Days of courtship.

November 10th The newspapers report that the Tories are pledged to setting us free, that they will govern a Britain with a devalued pound, a crumpled Empire, a Navy controlled by the USA, and a continuing saga of rationing and restrictions. Good luck to them. Maybe they should stroll around here sometimes in order to see how a few of their Westminster constituents living within the Division Bell area exist.

I often wish Henry, Roland's ageing and ailing father, could make the journey from Putney to have dinner with us. He has a home help three days a week, but I am sure he doesn't eat properly. He is so thin, with an obsession for tidying things up. I saw something similar once in a woman who had been trained in the art of dressing shop-windows. She couldn't help herself, picking fluff off the carpet, a piece of cotton or hair from a person's lapel, or rearranging objects to form new alignments; and Henry is the same. When Sally went with Roland to see him on Sunday, taking the bus to Putney Bridge, he sang as he opened the door: 'If I knew you were coming I'd have baked a cake, baked a cake', from a tune popular on the wireless at the moment.

Henry spends most of his daylight hours hunched over an Underwood typewriter, picking out the letters of his memoirs. He has known many fascinating people in his time, keeping copious notebooks. As a journalist he worked with both Hannan Swaffer and Arthur Conan Doyle, visiting St Petersburg before the Revolution and dancing, so he said, with Pavlova at a ball while teaching the young Karsavina how to Charleston.

There has been no word from Toby since the letter from Paris. He appears to have gone to ground somewhere on the Continent or, worse still, the Soviet Union. Ever since Burgess and Maclean left in June rumours have been circulating on the film set. Meanwhile, Roland is making full use of Toby's heavy tweed jacket with leather patches at the elbows, which he left behind on his last visit. He is wearing it with a black cashmere scarf wound round his neck, looking every inch the rogue-male to the raised tenement eyes.

November 22nd The Chancellor, the Right Hon. R. A. Butler, has announced that Britain is in danger of becoming bankrupt, idle and hungry. Life for us, however, goes on much the same. There was a joke on the wireless's Light Programme *Take It From Here*, which said:

'Have you seen Jim's new suit? It's the Conservative cut.'

'What's a Conservative cut?'

'The same as the Socialist cut, only they're more polite about it.'

Nationally, we should be picking up soon with the implementation of the new Education Act, the National Health Service, National Insurance Act and Town and Country Planning Act. Leafing through a June 1941 edition of *Picture Post* I read with interest an article on the New Britain: 'A Plan for Britain', the kind of land we were fighting for. The article ran beside an advert for slick Brylcreamed hair, which might help to achieve this new image we seek!

Belinda called again this evening under cover of darkness, huddled in an old coat. She had been crying. It seems the relationship is going through problems again. She says although committed to his wife in theory, he doesn't love her and suggests that he and Belinda leave it to Fate.

'I'm a great believer in Fate,' he is supposed to have told her. 'Leave it to Fate to work it out.' Which sounds to me like a man too caught up in the demands of marriage to do anything about it. Meanwhile, she says, he intends to keep himself busy with work. I have faith in Belinda and whatever is best for her will be.

I made her a cup of cocoa and two slices of toast. Walking later with her across the yard, window after window was lit as the tenement backdrop danced into life. My thoughts were concerned with tomorrow's dinner and the problem of what to have, rather than with Belinda and her woes, but I remain optimistic for her chances.

There was an hour to spare before Roland came back and bedtime, so I spread a length of material I had bought in the Army and Navy Stores Piecegoods Department over the table to cut out a pattern. Once the breakfast things are cleared away in the morning I can pin it together on my dressmaker's dummy and have it finished in no time.

November 25th The newspapers and BBC news are carrying reports of the threat of a Third World War, with Russia fighting the USA with her allies in Korea. I find this disturbing. The world and winter seem very removed from spring's glimpse of snowdrops, daffodils and wafer-thin leaves. And there is Christmas to get through first.

It is no better on our own doorstep. Ada Perkins and Annie Ward's mother were in the yard fighting over some nonsense or other this morning, kicking and punching one another as, encored and encouraged by a retinue of onlookers, they tore into the day. I went back indoors and climbed through the bedroom window to make an exit, lifting Sally down from the sill. I felt quite sick afterwards and did not return until nightfall.

I stitched a piece of grey astrakhan fur trimming on to the collar and cuffs of my old coat to give it a new lease of life. There was a bit left for a muff. The fur had been in my rag-bag since the day I took Patricia and Belinda, as children, to see the Lying-in-State of King George V. They had both worn little berets and muffs from the same fur.

Roland is in bed with acute bronchitis and every rasping cough and wheeze brings him closer to a stay in hospital, which he won't like. He has inherited Katrina's morbid and suspicious fear of hospitals and doctors. Where is that painterly vision now, I ask myself between those enervating coughs? I collected some thoughts together and placed them in a letter to Claudine, posting them in the Victoria Street Post Office box marked 'Country'. As I went across the yard Elsie and Alice Sugden, sisters of Joe, were coming in from Abbey Orchard Street. 'Good evening,' they said in unison. 'Looking forward to Christmas then?'

November 30th Sally gave Belinda's cardigan away the other night. She leans out of her bedroom window and offers her toys and items of clothing to whoever happens to be passing. She gave the cardigan to a girl called Sandra from Great Peter Street, who said she was cold. So will Belinda be cold without her cardigan. Then on Saturday I lost mine somewhere near Pont Street where I was hurrying for the No. 46 bus which was speeding down Sloane Street. I spent most of my week either sewing, mending or stitching to ensure the survival of our clothing. At this rate I will have to visit a few more jumble sales.

Roland came in tonight having rescued a pile of last year's yellowing editions of the *Westminster and Pimlico News* from the block entrance. In spite of a lingering smell of moth-balls, they made fascinating reading, informing us of interesting local snippets. For example, I had not realised the Salvation Army Hostel up the road in Great Peter Street had celebrated its fortieth birthday last year. The article said the hostel houses some 565 men nightly, provides over 10,000 meals a week and around 45,000 cups of tea a month. What a wonderful job it does. It seems that this home for millions of homeless men, the flotsam and jetsam of human life, had as its first officer-in-charge a local celebrity by the name of Old Macgregor. Formerly a vagrant, who had drunk by day and slept by night in a dustbin covered in newspapers, he had apparently undergone a change of heart, clothing and outlook to perform this important task brilliantly. A case of someone knowing the business from inside-out, as they say.

Despite the cold, Sally insisted on having one of those 1d distillations of sugar, cochineal and waterice, referred to as an Ice Lolly, from the market sweetshop. Just looking at it turned me a contrasting blue with the cold.

At the top of one of the blocks in the Little Square lives a lady tailoress, who I understand runs a profitable aside, transforming rags into skirts, jackets, caps and trousers. I admire anyone who can do this, removing grease and stains with a mixture of ammonia and other chemicals; concealing rents and tears to produce items which look as good as new. A hat, she told me, can be renovated by cutting the lower, greasy bottoms off. A second-hand silk hat can be recognised by the shortness of its crown. By ironing, brushing and combing what remains of the silk, it is made to lie smooth, with a selection of white ink, glue, paint, silk and brown paper to cover or hide the flaws left by time and wear.

Following pages   *We can only buy Utility furniture – it is all that is available – but at least our bedroom offers a chance of privacy.*

December 3rd I went to the doctor on Friday with my nerves. Roland and I barely communicate these days; this place, the noise in the streets, with mothers standing gossiping, casting doleful glances in our direction when we go past, is getting me down. I feel as though I am living in a goldfish bowl. The lack of privacy; the basic act of being able to use the WC in peace is impossible. There is always someone in there, or a queue forming on the other side of the door. This in royal, tourist-attraction Westminster. It is so humiliating. The doctor gave me a solution to relieve constipation: an affliction brought on by this hurried or avoided activity. It won't have been the first time I have gone out to use the public ones in the Army and Navy Stores, which are cleaner and afford a measure of privacy.

There has been a petition going round to have St Matthew's Street turned into an Official Playstreet. The noise is bad enough now. Its implementation would mean they would be out there day and night, including Sundays, yelling out to any prohibited motorist: 'Oi, mate. This is a Playstreet. Clear off!'

The street along which our block stands is some three hundred yards long. Before the Westminster Improvements of the 1880s, mooted by such notables as Lord Shaftesbury, Charles Dickens and Baroness Burdett-Coutts among others, this ground had built on it some seventy residences with 190 families and animals. Three thousand people in total. One can only wonder at those alleys and courts with their hours of gossip, talk and argument; the lives which were both vague and vivid, hurried and unhurried, uncompromising and vulture dark. We are living over them and their ghostly inhabitance. It is small wonder that one night I saw the form of an old woman with a fierce expression standing at the foot of the bed. I woke with a start, her ghostly image filling me with terror. I have never seen her since, thank God, and all I had the presence of mind to do was to make the sign of the Cross.

There has been a dreadful smell in the brickwork around the bedroom door for several days. A tenement workman had to knock part of the wall down, burrowing through the internal brickwork to expose the putrefying remains of a rat. He decided it had travelled up from the sewers which run beneath this pile and found a passage through the disintegrating mortar. Sewers? Rats? Whatever next? The thought of that rotting blackness lying beneath the floorboards, the stinking earth which has absorbed a century's secrets, filled me with horror and kept me awake at night for over a week. It is not only artists who have vivid imaginations.

December 18th Christmas will soon be here. The bomb site at the end of the market is in use again, with its seasonal displays of trinkets, plaster of Paris Santa Clauses, and coloured bells, trees and paperchains. We bought a few to decorate the room for Sally's benefit, as she now understands the meaning behind Christmas. I made some paper lanterns and we have hung them around the walls to hide the cracks and peeling distemper.

The woollens are taking ages to dry with the weather being so damp. The four o'clock post brought a set of complimentary tickets for the pantomine at the Chelsea Palace, so we will take Trixie with us as well. Maud from the dress shop has given me lengths of periwinkle-blue georgette and crêpe to make a matching dress and slip. She says that Petticoat Lane Market near Liverpool Street Station has many material bargains on Sunday mornings, and suggests I go with her one day. I might even find a few scraps to make Roland a couple of ties.

My black suede shoes need mending but, until I can afford it, a cardboard instep will do instead. I can't keep wearing peep-toe sandals in this wet weather, and my coat, in spite of the astrakhan trims, is virtually falling to bits. Roland insists that if we don't maintain some semblance of dignity in these impoverished times, we will be done for.

I have made out a Christmas card list, including the names of Mr Cornelius Wilby and his friend Mr Pashkoff in the Artillery Mansions, or 75 Victoria Street as they are sometimes called.

'After all,' said Roland, glancing down the names, 'Christmas is a time to forget one's worries, kick off one's shoes and go dancing down Old Pye Street.'

December 29th It is bitterly cold today, with a promise of rain. In spite of the fact that it is not yet Epiphany, I have already cleared away most of the Christmas decorations, which were getting on my nerves.

We came in tonight to observe a lone child sitting on the block entrance in the cold, eating a fragment of apple dipped in lemon sherbet, outlining her mouth with a yellow halo. A cartoon of a face, I thought, sitting there with her chapped hands and legs. What was she thinking, wondering? What will she be doing tomorrow when the winds have changed to sun? How will she feel, really feel, for one can never tell from the expression on their faces? We are so adept at concealing ourselves. What will we all be thinking and doing tomorrow for that matter?

'Have faith,' as Roland reminded me. 'Have faith. It's our beacon in the night.'

Then Ruby O'Keefe knocked at the door with a packet of Chesterfield cigarettes that some Yank called Robert had given her. Another one of her lone men friends, aimlessly working his way through London in search of amusement and the meanest caress to bring the year to a close.

THE GOLD
OF THE SUN

1952

January 1st Time is passing. Our lives are passing. Roland says that time is a gift, whichever side of it you are on. I think he meant that to cheer me up.

I was feeling a little restless, so at five o'clock I got up and made a cup of tea for myself. The early hours have a stillness about them which acknowledges my breathing. There is not a movement anywhere. No obvious sounds of the New Year's arrival. The car hooters sounded at midnight when the pub-crawlers were turned out, but little else. Leaving behind these streets set in shadows, in contrast to those of daylight. The room is quite bright, lit by an area of light on the ceiling cast by a street-lamp. In less than an hour June Flynn will be up to begin her paper round, and Ruby O'Keefe will be returning, less glamorous and available than in previous hours; and I will be putting the kettle on again for Roland to shave. He sleeps well, nothing really gets him down. He is lucky. January 1st will be like any other day for him, but for me it begins a year I am determined will be our last in the tenement.

Jean Farmer never wrote from Australia, and Charlie, who stayed behind after all that, transferred to Blackfriars on his own. It is the same with others who have left. Once they move, that seems to be the end of it. But then, one should never attempt to go back.

Belinda is getting on with her life, working by day as a florist and by night as a cashier in a club off Berkeley Street. Jim set her up in the florist shop as his way of maintaining contact with her until 'Fate' resolves the problems for them.

'I love him and he loves me,' she said, and that was that. Roland says love is a longing to hold, to possess. That it is not possible to love, really love, someone who is not longed for.

'That is fondness and attachment, but not desire or love,' he says.

I only worry that she is not seeing the situation with Jim clearly, for sometimes we can look at a person closely and not really see them. We fail to observe the continuity of mood. So much disillusionment comes from infatuation with things and people.

It is going to be cold today, with a hint of rain, the Home Service News warned. I feel cold in spite of the fire's warm embers. Roland still talks about the war and the period leading up to it. Dominic said it was an escape from the present, like acting.

There is someone about at last, drawing water from the tap. It sounds like Bessie Fonseca walking with her hollow step to rinse her yellowing teeth. Bang goes the street-door to wake everyone else. That's her all right! Thinking fondly of Belinda, I remembered some lines I read in a book:

> *When love is right*
> *It stays*
> *Filling, fulfilling*
> *Freeing one from*
> *Oneself.*

January 16th Sally is starting to get curious about her environment. She cannot understand why the kids around here are so hostile towards her, nor why they poke their tongues out and call her names. If I let her play outside they will torment her so she has to remain indoors with her toys and hobbies. I don't always have the energy to take her to the park, especially when it is so cold. Life can be difficult for an only child. They have to learn early on to draw strength from inner resources. Before she arrived I had a boy, stillborn at five months, whom we would have called James. Since Sally there has been the other miscarriage, which the doctor believes to be the root cause of my melancholia.

Sally spends hours with her chalks, crayons and scraps of paper, drawing. I give her the inside wrappings from empty tea-packets to use as tracing paper, or card from inside Shredded Wheat boxes. The priest says she has definite talent. She gets her creative streak from Roland and her ability to make things from scraps from me. In time, I hope, we will leave here and her life will become an open picture-frame full of opportunities into which she can step. It might help make up for this desolate start.

We had tea with Mr Pashkoff again today in Dickens Café, with me looking resplendent in a refurbished black-velvet costume.

'The three duties of a woman', he said, quoting from Somerset Maugham, 'are to be pretty, well dressed and never to contradict.'

I am not sure whether he was making a statement or offering advice. Either way, we shared a good pot of tea to accompany a plate of Vienna cakes. As one grows older, one becomes more silent, I suppose. Certainly Roland has already retired from the world to build one of his own.

At least the ducks seemed happy on the lake in St James's Park in their search for food. In spite of the weather and the threat of smog, we did go there for a walk after all. We left at about the same time Princess Elizabeth and the Duke of Edinburgh left for a tour in the sunshine of East Africa, Australia and New Zealand.

February 2nd I bought a tin of this new Nescafé Coffee Powder today. As with the Maxwell House, one adds a teaspoonful to nearly boiling water, with a little milk and sugar to provide, so the ad. says, 'coffee with a roaster-fresh fragrance and flavour.' It did make a pleasant change from cocoa and tea, but I can't see it catching on.

Dominic is home for a while, staying with Henry in Putney. He spent most of last year travelling with a circus as a Musical Director and Master of Ceremonies, touring Ireland and Northern England with them. Dominic can turn his hand to anything, helping to put the Big Tent up, designing their posters and driving wagons full of lions and tigers all over the country. He survives, he says, on café fry-ups, bread and cheese, and sleeping on a camp bed in a caravan. Through his adventures, Dominic has become an astute observer of personality, amusing us with odd turns of phrase as he recalled anecdotes from circus life. He had seen Ruby on her way out, all furs, flowing hair and glittering baubles.

'She's certainly very glamorous. She'd make a good trapeze artist. I wonder if she's tied up with the Messina brothers? They're around her route.'

'Perhaps that is who Uncle Charles is,' I suggested.

Dominic had arrived bearing gifts, with a bottle of wine, a stick of French bread and a tin of chicken bought in a Soho Delicatessen. We had nothing in particular to celebrate so we toasted his return, as I piled the cups and saucers into the bowl and lit the gas under the kettle.

February 6th The news today is very sad. Our beloved King George VI has died in his sleep. The wireless newscaster said that people were crying in the streets because they felt they had lost a personal friend. Death often reveals how real and accepted a love has been.

If the hours of today have seemed flat or uneventful, a private day of thoughts and secrets, then the night ones took on an even larger aspect. A sober inhabitance which was curtained and contained.

> *Wondering free and alone*
> *As dusk hangs on the horizon*
> *Moonlight pushing through*
> *The trees. Is this reality?*
> *The King is dead.*
> *God Bless the Queen.*

February 12th We still like to walk along the Embankment opposite where they held the Festival of Britain last year. We never went because we couldn't afford to go, but it was pleasant to watch the festivities, the fireworks and dancing from this side of the Thames. The excitement seemed to waft over together with the 'Fun, fantasy and colour' promised by Gerald Barry, the Festival's Director-General. We liked the red, white and blue awnings, the flags and bunting which helped lift the gloom and perimeter haze effected by the weather, gaslight and fog. The shop-windows still display photographs of our new Queen and her Consort, often with ribbon sashes draped over them. For those with an eye for line and colour, there is plenty of stimulus around. The Festival of Britain evoked a happy period, the extended party which has helped to wash away the war and years of deprivation. Everyone seemed to be a little sad when it ended. We still have Battersea, the Funfair and Pleasure Gardens with its Guinness Clock and Tree Walk.

Sally has a new admirer in Fabrizzio, who, wearing a continual five-o'clock shadow, makes sandwiches at Costa's Café next to the Artillery Mansions in Victoria Street. Handing her a 2d ice-cream cornet out of the window-hatch, he enlivens her imagination with tales of the Mardi Gras with its gypsies, processions and pierrots. 'One day I take you,' he says.

February 15th At 2 p.m. today a silence fell over Westminster. The cries of the stallholders in Strutton Ground were stilled; the street buses and taxis were halted, and the children bid to stand beside their desks in memory of our late King.

I took Sally and Trixie to the King's Lying-in-State in Westminster Hall to pay our last respects. It has been a purple day. A sad occasion with thousands of heads bent in prayer, as we slowly filed past. Trixie said she had heard the news at school when her class's *Music and Movement* lesson had been interrupted with it.

I bought a souvenir edition of *Picture Post* magazine; the main story presented the King's demise as the passing of an age, suggesting that he had brought a quality of dignity and graciousness to the Crown. He will be greatly missed.

It got dark very early today. In fact the damp fogginess has blighted what little light we did have for most of the day. We made our way back gingerly, walking from gas-lamp to gas-lamp, street into street, with Sally holding Trixie's hand, and me hers. Roland was at his notes when we came in. I had not expected him to be home so early.

'Death is the only thing any of us can be certain of in this life,' he said. 'When I was a child I believed God was everywhere, if not always in the person. I would talk to the trees and place the leaves to my ears like a telephone receiver, expecting to hear His voice.'

'And did you?'

'Oh yes. Many times. But it is not always what you want to hear.'

'It's what He doesn't say that you should listen to,' I added. 'What has made you remember this now?'

'The thought that life continues in spite of us. That our life and contribution to it is so minute in the greater scheme of things.'

He's absolutely right, I thought. Life isn't even a respecter of kings. I left him with his notes, returned Trixie to her mother and put the potatoes on to boil. It was herrings again, rolled in flour and oatmeal, and boiled cabbage. Sally helped me lay the table, spreading out the red-and-white cloth, placing the cruet, cutlery and bottle of Chef's Tomato Ketchup.

We ate in silence. Even Sally seemed to be unusually subdued. I consoled myself that spring was around the corner, along with Sally's first term at school. We may well opt for the Burdett-Coutts and Townshend Foundation C. of E. Primary School, with special instruction in her faith from the priest. And Roland can ensure her understanding of the catechism.

But it remains a deep indigo night as the costers leave for Covent Garden. Dominic, paying us another of his lightning visits, said we should circulate more and be circulated, as we are in danger of becoming remote. He made us sound like an old photograph in need of enlargement.

March 1st It rained all day today, loosening the gutters and yard of some of the dirt. I left the washing for another day, as it would never dry in this. The walls are sweating with condensation; trickles of water running down in worm-like threads over their surfaces. When a kettle boils one can't see for steam; the concrete passages are damp as well, with darkening distemper and 30-watt electricity bulbs. It is strange how the landings have electric lighting and the rooms gas. Interminable, exhausting and essentially destructive are these maggots burrowing through this century-old pile, this darkened beast of a pile, which runs through the nether side of Westminster.

Like a March hare with a March wind behind him, the Monsignor called again today, with another four visits to make in this block alone. Roland was in this time, offering him a glass of tonic wine, which was all we had. He was so polite he didn't even flinch. 'He'd make a good actor,' said Roland later.

I think he is one already, performing when the stage is lit. A pose maintained for the duration of the Credo, prayers of petition, Offertory and Act of Consecration, cloaked in crimson, emerald or white vestments, according to the Octave. He no doubt lives through the week for those Masses, with face composed as the man who perceives truth.

I found myself wondering at his day and how different it must be from ours. 'It will be ordered, very ordered,' said Roland. In my mind's eye I could see him rising, brushing his teeth, covering his face with shaving cream before buttoning his collar, and drinking his first cup of tea. An elderly housekeeper, probably a po-faced Sister of Mercy, would have been up an hour before him to leave his cup on a tray outside his door. I could almost see him, visualise his lovely face as he made his way through the Sacristy to open the church door, where the old ladies would be waiting. Standing like puppets with their individual smells of age, moth-balls, sleep and decay. They would all be there: the gossips, their petty jealousies and arguments over, collecting the hymn books, cleaning the candle-stands, or rearranging the altar flowers. I shuddered for him. Shuddered for myself and my image of a man who would never have someone to reach for in the night; for the thought of his hours ahead.

'You won't have been the first to convert to Catholicism through falling in love with a priest,' said Roland, giving me a wink while interpreting my thoughts. Indeed I wouldn't, I thought. The Monsignor would be very easy to fall in love with, if only for his simple gaze and quiet humility. If I found him attractive so would others, those who would follow him with their eyes hoping for signs of approval or recognition with a variety of ploys aimed towards his vulnerability.

When Roland went out later for a walk I remembered how rough these streets were a century ago. Ada Kinsella from one of the lodging houses, a seventy-two-year-old who was educated at St Stephen's School in Rochester Row, said that people were afraid to walk down Great Peter Street at night.

'It had two lodging houses: Aunt Charlotte's for women; and Pat Riley's for men.'

Thinking of all those ghosts around Bennett's Yard and Laundry Yard, the squalor of Carpenter's Street, Ann's Place and Blue Anchor Court, the news that it used to be dangerous does not surprise me.

March 3rd We made do with a meal of mutton and boiled potatoes tonight. Roland declared he is going to become a vegetarian. The next time he turns his nose away in disgust I will give his dinner to Old Irish. I bet she would be glad of it. But I know he doesn't mean it. He manages to keep busy the same as I do, filling in the hours with this and that. He stays in more these nights, playing board games with Sally and Trixie, Ludo or Snakes and Ladders. He has been teaching Sally how to read in readiness for next term. I have made her a little black shoe-bag with a drawstring and her name embroidered over it. I noticed all the cloakroom pegs had one hanging from them when I went to see the Headmistress last month. Sally will be in Class 5 at the far end of the ground floor; a room filled with tiny desks and chairs, a blackboard and table for the teacher. It looks as formal a setting as when I was at school in the late Twenties. The classroom was warmed by a large open fireplace with a guard in front. The junior part of the school is on the floor above, and the top floor, which once included children from eleven to thirteen plus, was badly damaged during the war. When it is eventually rebuilt, they will have a playground on the roof.

Whenever Roland goes to Stiles the Bakers for bread, or to George the Greengrocer for firewood, he is referred to as 'Guv'. Even the coalman delivering our weekly hundred-weight to the coal cupboard calls him this. 'OK Guv' or 'All right Guv', which he sees as an old-fashioned term for expressing respect without subservience, in the market kingdom of coster, spiv and barrow-boy.

For the record, I did a spot-check on Strutton Ground in order to list the shops and businesses there for posterity.

We have a Fishmonger, Kennedy's the Grocer's, Tobacconist, Newsagent's, Radio and Electrical Shop, the Golden Pen Shop, Rhodes Restaurant, Pearks, Blackwell's Drug Store, the Dairy, Harris Newsagents, Wood Merchant's, Hairdresser's, Café, Butcher's, Grocer's, Jeweller's, Vaughan's Chemist, Shoe Repairs, Lipton's, Fruit Basket, Haberdasher's, United Dairy, Stiles the Bakers, Littlewood's the Ironmonger's, along with barrows selling fruit, flowers and vegetables, and assorted items.

From this list one can see that we are comprehensively served by the market, with little need to wander further afield. I like to, though, because shopping in the Army and Navy Stores or Warwick Way offers a change of scenery that I need.

The Abbey end of Victoria Street, near Dean's Yard.

March 6th The women's magazines still give advice on how to style hair and generally make the most of oneself, especially with the use of Home Permanents. I haven't tried one since the last attempt and have let it grow a little. I haven't really changed my hairstyle since 1940, when the fashion was to wear curls in the front with the side bits held back with combs. Poor Mr Waghorn in the workroom at the time was so surprised. 'Whatever have you done with your hair?' he said. 'You've spoilt a pretty face!'

It is very cold today. I took Sally and Mr Putney for a walk across Green Park towards Piccadilly to make a change. We were both well wrapped against the wind. We had a look at the more glamorous reaches of London; the London of the Ritz, Jackson's the Grocer's, and Fortnum and Mason. One can dream sometimes. Dreams of how it could be. I felt quite good walking among those shopping in floor-length mink coats. At this time of the year one feels as though the sun will never shine again.

According to a special survey carried out by the Ministry of Education's Inspectors into the sanitary conditions in some of the Westminster schools, Westminster is a 'black spot'. The report criticised the sites, decoration, caretaking, classrooms, lighting and heating, equipment, furniture and cloakroom facilities. The only items left out of the criticism were the staff and children. We can assume they are above that.

Salley and Mr Putney.

April 3rd With Easter on the horizon I bought a few chocolate eggs wrapped in shiny paper from a market stall, and a bottle of cochineal to dye our Easter-morning boiled eggs. We sat round the kitchen table with scissors, a paste of flour and water, card, coloured gummed-paper and a few sequins to make home-made Easter cards. Sally produced a bunny rabbit, Roland an Easter bonnet, Trixie a bunch of flowers and I a simple Cross surrounded by daisies. I love these evenings of activity and occupation, listening to the wireless, enjoying the extra evening light of British Summer Time. Even the noise in St Matthew's Street fails to intrude on these occasions.

In the local paper the Warwick Way Bargain Centre was advertising a range of goods at reduced prices. I came home with a liberty bodice priced 6d for Sally, a pair of pyjamas for Roland at 4/6d, a petticoat for 1/6d and a pair of Wellington boots for 3/6d. Passing a radio and electrical shop on the way home, I noticed a nine-inch Bush television set in the window for a mere 49 guineas. I think we can give that a miss for the time being.

I have a feeling that we won't be seeing or hearing from Toby again, nor discover how his affair with Violette is progressing. Roland thinks she was a KGB spy, and that, on reflection, Toby was himself working clandestinely for both the East and the West, and had probably done so since Cambridge.

I bought a bunch of white chrysanthemums. Mrs Banks upstairs said white flowers in the house keep bad spirits away. Maybe they do and maybe they don't, but they certainly help to brighten the khaki distemper.

Maurice-the-Milk in the Playfoot Dairy said yesterday that we have a lot to be thankful for. Sally and I were having a sandwich lunch in there and couldn't help overhearing his voice above everyone else's. He is absolutely right. We have a roof over our heads, food, albeit restricted, and our health. We are survivors in this tenement. Survivors inspired and influenced by the collective anonymity of our lives.

April 16th Roland has gone for a walk up the Charing Cross Road to look in the shop-windows of the various gentlemen's outfitters. He says that it is one of his favourite streets, with its own brand of tumbling, late nineteenth-century tenements, bookshops and a few recently opened coffee and milk bars. The bustle of this street shouldering Leicester Square and Shaftesbury Avenue reminds him of his childhood, when he walked along Broadway in Manhattan. The street with its smells, which give the mind so intimate a register. With little more than the price of a cup of tea in his pockets, Roland could still acknowledge the pulse and rhythm of the city, which Westminster denies him.

Sally had a surprise today with an unexpected gift: a game of draughts and a bottle of Tizer from Freddie, who cycled over on his bicycle. She has even taken to drinking an occasional cup of Camp Coffee, especially when made the special way by Henry at Putney. Special way means that he puts an extra spoonful of sugar in the cup. Mr Putney has to have a cup too in a tiny red teaset Mother bought her from Woolworth's.

April 22nd There is a sadness when, looking for a fondly remembered street, café or shop, you discover that it has gone. This is one of passing time's yardsticks. The street-lamps and corner shops, the ice-cream man and coffee stall; character scenes from a postcard awaiting our return. All it takes is a tune or a pungent aroma to bring the memory back. Even the war has a certain poignancy now, like reading a loved one's letter after death. When the images of darkened, blistered buildings and the waterless fountains in Traflagar Square enlarge one's soul.

During a still moment I sometimes look through Roland's notes. 'Art gives visibility to things which matter. It is not enough to simply reproduce,' I read. 'The duty of the artist is to spread truth as he sees it.'

It is five o'clock and I am sitting lost in concentration. The smell of a fruit cake baking in the oven and the vase of yellow narcissi on the sill bring me back to reality. To get some air I go to the block entrance with the pretext of shaking the tablecloth free of crumbs. The yard is crowded. A few of the kids are circling on roller-skates in and out of the pigeons. Few listen to *Children's Hour* on the wireless or to *Dick Barton, Special Agent*. Casting a quick glance over the blocks, the stone walk-up entrances and iron railings, the row of pram-sheds, lace curtains and old women sitting on hard-backed chairs defines this interlude precisely. Returning to our room I opened the window to let in some air. A game of rounders is in progress amid a multitude of shrieks and cries. There are a few letters to write, the floor to sweep. How long will it last, this dance? Will we get a change of partners for our dancing? I hope so.

Spotted like diamonds
The daisies around the
Lake, stand beyond the
Leaves.

Out of work and bored,
the street-corners seem
the best place to
see the world.

May 12th Florrie Banks from the fourth floor came in to read my tea-leaves the other night, carefully sifting through the formation of leaves. Mrs Dodds said I should ask her to read them because she would bring us luck.

'You want to get out of here, don't you?' she asked. 'But you won't just yet. Your husband isn't very strong. He won't live a long life. He lives on his nerves.'

She was right. Roland does smoke too much, living mostly on cups of sweet tea and roll-up cigarettes, which he taps ceremoniously on his silver cigarette case before lighting up. He spends so much of his time magnetised and traumatised by those erstwhile thoughts which embroider his notebooks. Escaping reality, exchanging the West End where, he says, he feels alone and yet part of. Florrie also said that he won't have left me much behind except for his friendship. She was wrong there. He will have left me Sally.

That evening when he came in, and for some unknown motive, he put on his yellow bow-tie, the one I made him before the war to go with the Mustard-Dog Pup he had kept since childhood. It was an uncanny attempt at a celebration in this domicile of a thousand sighs and a glass of tonic wine. A domicile so dark we have to go into the street to look for the space which makes possible the sun's reflection. He even bought Sally a bag of bull's eyes and some aniseed balls. I simply busied myself in the cupboard, folding out those gingham-like bread wrappings for his morning marmalade sandwiches, ever mindful of Florrie's predictions.

'You'll marry again. You'll see,' she said.

'The bulldozer will be coming to this area soon,' Roland said later, out of the blue. 'To split this oasis right down the middle. I've heard a rumour that this environment of ours will have disappeared in a few years. Victoria Street, all those little alleys, courts, mansion blocks and shops. Nothing will remain to remind the world of this world.

'But I bet this pile will remain,' he added, thumping the wall. 'When they built these, like their inhabitants they were meant to last.'

I wondered if he had sensed Florrie's presence and had known that she had read my tea-leaves.

'That's when we will look back on this time with a sense of nostalgia,' I said. 'Will come to regard it as a period of optimism, innovation and movement, forgetting the hourly hardship, the uncertainty, lack of money, neighbourhood closeness and noise.'

Outside in the street a thin blue light outlined a cat passing over the concrete. Its markings meeting the movement, as life and sleep contorted into the next watchful hour.

May 20th I think it true that most of us never reach our own sense of happiness: never achieve a glimpse of the true gold of the sun. I would like to think Roland and I have brought one another a little joy, companionship, the hand to reach for in the dark, but happiness I don't think so. He grumbles if there is no sugar left for his tea, no crease in his trousers, while I sit with a stomach which feels tight. We talk, provide a chasm for the mind's solitude, but we go past one another. One has to go through things even when afraid of the dark and let go of the journey which has gone past its destination. The ducks on the lake look happy enough, eager for the child's tossed mosaics of bread.

I had better go and clear away the breakfast things, I suppose, otherwise I shall be late for work.

May 24th There was a coster's funeral in the street today for one of the matriarchs in the lodging houses. At the final count, there were thirty-one hearses with black horses, with carts filled with wreaths and flowers. The passing of an old woman marked, in a sense, the passing of a way of life and age.

The time is getting on and I have finished the ironing. There isn't anything much on the wireless, so I might as well go to the dress shop and see if there are any alterations to do. With the warmer days here again the work might pick up. I hope so. While I was in Warwick Way I bought a bottle of salad cream, lettuce, watercress, radishes, tomatoes and a tin of pilchards for tea. My sister Claudine is expecting her first child in June, which will be a cause for celebration. I have been knitting several matinée jackets for her, and have run up a few nighties for the new arrival. Sally can't wait to see her new baby cousin and hopes it will be a girl. We went to the park again this afternoon with a bag of stale bread for the ducks. Mr Hinton was feeding Peter and Paul the pelicans as we stood on the suspension bridge and watched.

The view across the lake was magnificent with its transforming alchemy of bronze and gold. Those seasonal vapours which are so brilliant it takes one's breath away.

I will make up Roland's marmalade sandwiches for tomorrow and get his cup of Horlicks ready with two cream crackers. He takes a laxative pill rolled in a twist of paper every other night before going to bed; and each Sunday night Sally has a spoon of California Syrup of Figs. Then I think I will have an early night. I have no idea where Roland is. Since the brighter evenings arrived he has been going out again in a swoop of mood which blasts him through the traffic, neon and crowds, when the blights of the hour get him down. Although he can probably be found sipping a solitary cup of tea in a West End café, or propped against the Embankment coffee stall beside Waterloo Bridge.

May 31st Changes are coming. Next year the tenement is going to be wired for electricity. One by one these tiny cell-like clusters of rooms will have, as Sally graphically puts it: 'Corners we can see into.'

There is already a van in the yard advertising All-Electric Homes, complete with a row of electric cookers one can go in to view. I will stay with gas because I know where I am with that. And, as Kathy next door says, if things get too bad one can always put one's head in the oven!

Then it will be the Coronation, the crowning of our young Queen Elizabeth at Westminster Abbey. There was a notice in the Rent Office declaring that from now, each Saturday morning, the porters and punters will be in the yard organising raffles, jumble sales and various other fund-raising events, to contribute towards next year's tenement street party, dances, souvenirs and entertainment. Sally can't wait and wants me to make her a red-white-and-blue dress for the occasion. We will be in the thick of it here. A mere stone's throw from the pageantry, populus and pantomime.

I had to laugh last night when it was rumoured that Old Irish had lost a ten-shilling note in the yard on her way home from the off-licence. When Roland went out later he recalled seeing half the block out in attitudes of prayer, looking for it. Later we learned she hadn't really lost it at all, but had merely misplaced it; found it on the kitchen table. I bet she enjoyed a good laugh at the tenants' expense.

Old Irish.

Another month has ended, bringing my favourite month into focus. I tidied up my assortment of pots, lipsticks and creams on the dressing table, and polished the mirror, placing the postcard of Venice back in the drawer. I put on a floral printed dress newly ironed, my sling-back sandals, tied my hair back in a bow and went for a walk along Victoria Street. The sunlight was catching the tops of the buildings, throwing the north side into shadow. It was a night and day street with its light and dark sides, bustling shops and people hurrying to their destinations; attempting to escape the darkness into the sun. The buses passed me on my side in the direction of Victoria, Sloane Square and Pimlico. A sandwich-board man whistled: 'Maybe it's because I'm a Londoner,' and I smiled at him. The balloon man was there, resplendent in a red-white-and-blue trilby. So were the newspaper vendor, the flower lady and window cleaner, threading their way through the daytime hours. Each blinking in the pale sun.

Roland suggested we go to Brighton on Sunday and enjoy a day by the sea. Let the wavering cadences of sea-water float over our faces; take a thermos of tea, sandwiches and munch pewter-toned pebbles and seaweed washed with the tide. We could buy a stick of rock, ice-cream and candy floss, link hands with summer's children over the other side of the Channel.

I disentangled my thoughts from my newspaper, drank my coffee and crossed over into the sun. There are changes coming. Plans to annihilate our Victorian inheritance; erase this area with its shabby gentility by a single flick of a chameleon's tongue. We are our landscape, are responsive to its spirit, the indistinguishable pulls of our heritage. I love this street with its colour-dashed tones of roan, heliotrope, salt-ash, soot and grime. Whose daytime brilliance is so in contrast with the evenness of night.

June 2nd A year from today it will be the Coronation. The Crowning of our new Queen Elizabeth the Second at Westminster Abbey. As we live so close to the activities we will be able to watch the preparations, the tourists and jollity as it builds up. Even the BBC Television are planning to monitor her route almost on our doorstep.

With the installation of electricity I will be able to have a small bedside reading lamp for the first time. Freddie said he would make me one using a raffia-based Chianti bottle with a shade from Woolworth's as our contribution to the New Contemporary Look. But until then I will continue to use a 1d candle at night.

The years are passing, quickly leaping over the discordance in our lives and the legacy of anxiety left from the war. It will be interesting to recall how much of this period remains on the surface of life. How many of its blocks, with their iron-chained staircases and people-density will continue in this throbbing Westminster world. Where these grey brick piles emulate Baudelaire's symbolistic forest, where people watch trees watching people, as the century-old mortar gradually encircles and takes over our lives.

I buy Sally a vanilla ice-cream wafer and a copy of the *Evening Star*; watching the man place the wafers and ice-cream into the mould before flicking it over to hand it to her. We walk home hand in hand past the woman scrubbing her front step, and the old man blowing his nose into an envelope. Moving past the children riding scooters and tricycles, while a mongrel dog barks at its reflection in a shop window. Cutting across the bomb site littered with silver paper, broken biscuits, tins, cigarette packets and rags, my foot comes to rest against an old boot.

Mrs Streetwatcher, who from her window spends her entire days and most of her nights watching those who have not the time, not the interest to watch her.

Opposite   *Coronation Day party, 2nd June 1953.*

Sally helps me lay the table with a special place for Mr Putney. Roland won't be back until later, so I sit for a moment with my eyes closed against the evening sun streaming through the window, silhouetting the blitzed remains of the Mission Hall of the Good Shepherd opposite.

I have a historical romance to read. They are calling us the New Elizabethans. This book is about the first ones and some of their problems are not very different from ours. Costa's, the Italian café in Victoria Street, has changed its name to the New Era Restaurant and has stopped selling ice-cream cornets. A New Era. Will it be for us? Perhaps it will. I hope so.

> *Saffron sky tipped with silver*
> *A lime-jade dust settles*
> *Over the streets*